WORDS DO FAIL

PROMISES MADE, WORDS SPOKE,
ASSURANCES GIVEN - EVERYTHING SEEMS
TO FAIL WITH TIME

NIKHIL

Made with ♥ on the Notion Press Platform
www.notionpress.com

The book is dedicated to the person who came into my life
at an early age and made me know the true meaning of
love, life, and promises. Who left and made me realize the
importance of waiting for someone. It returned to my life
and made me believe in the power of hope.
Who taught me the power of pain.
I may not have given what was promised to her. I could
not speak to her, but I promised to keep loving her and be
there for her.
I dedicate this book wholeheartedly to her love and care.

Contents

FOREWORD

The story is a work of fiction inspired by incidents happening around me. The society around us doesn't always seem the same as we grow up. It hides itself when we are a child and reveals its true nature as we grow.
The story is about true love, where promises are being made, words are exchanged about the future, their life together, and whatnot, and assurances are being made to each other. Perfect True love it is. But in the end, it all fails to stand. And the reason for the failure was not the pair who was deeply in love; the mistake was not of the people but the society. Of course, society is made of people, made of tradition, followed blindly for centuries, with no one to question or think about their impact on the lives of individuals and the harm it is creating to everyone.
The story explains the emotions of a helpless individual who is deeply in love with his girl, his princess but faces one of the strongest situations of realizing reality. When his self-confidence fails to support him, his family becomes a burden, and his love becomes an obstacle.

PREFACE

The book aims to bring the reality of society, how it makes young people believe in love and, ultimately, break those promises. The motive is to make people understand the struggle individuals go through in selecting between their family and society on one side and their true love on the other. Both are equally important to them and cannot be selected together.

A Painful Puzzle that is destined to hurt.

I

A Deep Thought

Life looks so different today. A different view about the things I have come across, or precisely the things I have faced and come out with. From childhood, I heard people tell me about the miracles and lessons life would teach me. I was made to believe in everything, calmly listened to every story, and never thought that the experience would be more demanding than detailed in the reports told.

Stories are fictional, and they were told to us at an age when we were not in a position to find the difference between unreal illusion and reality.

But one question about the past just popped into my head. Why did no one teach me how to face these situations, and why is every elder busy explaining the fictional unreal stories to us? Why are people proud of the challenges they face but, at the same time, fail to tell people how to meet or fight with them?

We proud Indians have grown up hearing the fantasies our grandparents make us listen to. At late midnight look at the open dark sky, believing that all those fantasies and stories are true. Slowly and unknowingly imagined my own story with my role in it and closed my eyes to enter into those dreams, only to wake up in the morning to face reality.

One day when I was a child, I was depressed for one of the million reasons we used to get depressed those days. And I was sitting in front of my house looking at the plants in front of my home, enjoying the peaceful loneliness. My grandfather approached me and sat next to me, observing the sad look on my face and understanding that I was miserable. I still remember what my grandfather, who is in his 70s, spoke about how difficult it will be when you lose hope. He spoke about the difficulties that he faced in life and how hard life was for him. He once had four sons and three daughters. Unfortunately, he lost one of his sons only a few months after the birth. Even before the family recovers from this loss, another blow hits the family. His elder son, who had recently got a prestigious job, as quoted by my grandfather very Proudly, has a significant health situation in which his neck nerves became weak, and he cannot keep his head straight.

He said, "My son has had a difficult time. He once got a prestigious job, and getting a job was difficult in those days. Nevertheless, he worked hard to achieve that position. Then that news was so warm for us in the middle of our depression after losing my newborn son only a few months back. But happiness is short-lived when my son got this unexpected health situation that he still suffers from."

My grandfather travelled to many hospitals, hoping to recover his son and see him as normal as before. But all his efforts brought no results. And I can still see my uncle suffering from that problem, and I never wondered why he had that condition. He had lost his job. He is living separately along with his wife, surviving on the Pension provided by the government.

Looking at the situation in his life, other problems I faced seemed so small. My grandfather has never given up on life. He never gave up on hope. This is a lesson to be learned, but at that point my age, I could only enjoy listening and enjoying but never spent much time learning something from those lectures. I had no wisdom yet to understand the inferences from those life stories.

He used to tell what people told him about those situations.

""People used to say there is a bad curse on our family, and a pooja is to be performed to get out of the things that happen.""

"I don't want to take a chance. So your grandmother and I visited many temples and performed numerous rituals, leaving nothing left, keeping all the hope we had in every ritual. But the result of all those prayers is not seen till now. But I know one thing for sure. All these bad curses on the family and pooja things are to satisfy ourselves. So one thing is sure all these difficulties are a part of life. And no matter what, you have to face them".

That was a long lecture for a kid like me then. But I still see him waiting for that miracle to happen when he can see his elder son back to normal again. Maybe he is always sure that his son will not recover, but he never stops hoping and trying his best, leaving no stone untouched.

"Life is all about hope. No one is sure of anything, and the only thing everyone is doing is just hoping for something to happen."

Everyone in this world is good at sharing the problematic experiences they faced. They feel proud of the way they faced those difficulties. But no one taught me how to meet them. It is always thought that talking about problems is a rational thing. But it is only now I realize that this is the most foolish thing people judge wrongly.

Each person, a man who is a father to children, teaching them lessons of his life, a mother who cuddles her tiny baby, telling her to be vital to face life's challenges, all faced different problems in life. And yet most of them always fail to make their children face the realities when they grow up.

The problem with everyone is not the difficulties faced by each one, and it is that they are not well informed about life and are not prepared accordingly. They are not told the truths of society, and they believe only the fantasies that are said to them and in which they imagined their life.

How relatable the small piece looks at right. Relate it to your childhood and your adult or young age. All our childhood revolves around the stories in which we dream, with us playing the hero role of having a well and perfect life. We believe everything that was told.

We believe in friendship, we feel Love, we believe the truth, and we even believe lies are a bad thing in life.

But it is very late when we realize friendship fails to stand when money enters, Love fails to stand when caste and other differences enter, and the Importance of Truth and lies changes with changing our perception. The truth may be a lie for the other person, and a lie may be the truth to someone. It is the situation that determines everything, and when you reach that particular situation, It will be too late to realize.

I believed in Love more than anything. I fell in Love early in my childhood, which has changed my life in many ways, from motivating me to study harder to finally losing hope in everything. It has shown the fool inside me, the reality of society, and the cover on people's faces, who generally speak hundreds of things. But when it comes to implementations, words do fail to stand always.

I had never thought I would decide to let go of her. I never imagined that I could not achieve my life, career, and Love together. Thought in all the stories I have dreamed of right from my childhood, nothing worked in reality. So connecting the accounts with the world's facts isn't very reasonable. But why is it so?

Why the stories that are told to the children are just fantasy? Why can't they be true? Or why not only the reality of those stories compared to real lives said to the children?

In the middle of these stories and the morals taught to me exist the seeds of my feelings toward that girl. Nothing is wrong with having feelings for a girl if you like her. And frankly, I never cared to explain or thought about my feelings towards her.

But the truth is that all those no-restriction feelings are only for stories, and there is a thin border between the stories told, the morals taught, and the reality of life on the ground.

Before you realize the difference and find the thin borderline between these things, you are already late, suffering from pain and unable to find a way out. In such conditions, you will lose hope in life, you will lose hope in society, and you'll find yourself stuck in the middle of nowhere to go.

But there comes the primary lesson of life. It is time you take the learning of the things that happened and move on.

Society has lost its morals somewhere unknown in life's journey, and it will keep losing the game of energy all the time. Even in any success story, society is not at the forefront. Every success story of moral and ethics that we are taught about are mostly fantasy and made us believe to be accurate by telling them at an age we cannot find and those imprinted on our blank brains.

Throwback to when we are supposed to learn the thing we will follow for a generation's time. This is the time that everyone can use to train these minds with the things that can closely resemble the reality of the world. But in doing such things, fantasies took the primary hand.

Love happened to me at an early stage of life. Love is what shaped my life, and it has a very considerable effect on the choices I make in life.

Today I sit on the first floor of my house after resigning from my job, which I got after a lot of hard work, with no idea of what life has for me in the future and no thought of what I will do further. Just one thing with me at present is the depression caused by losing my Love. A foolish decision has brought me to the situation I am in now.

Not all decisions are significant, but very few make your life up and down. You never know which decision those are. You realize once the impact is felt.

Decisions are being taken thinking about our present temporary comfort of ours. But the impact of many of that decisions will be felt for years. I realized this late, and I find myself still making decisions considering my temporary comfort of mine.

Now, this has been chasing me for many weeks. This was when I was supposed to pursue my life, following my dreams and fulfilling them. But here I am, leaving the job with no other option and grieving the loss of my Love.

Facing this situation is very new to me. I know that this has to be faced strongly. But I feel the depression is wholly and slowly taking control of my mind and body. Maybe it is what forced me to resign from my job, may it is what collapsed all my dreams of achieving something great, or perhaps it is what blocked all my thoughts with no sight of my future in the near end.

For eight years, I have been in love with her. 8 years and still love her, but we are not together and will not be together, the thought of which is killing me from inside and outside. We dreamed about our life together for a long time,e as long as we are on this planet. But all my dreams are collapsed by one person, none other than myself, responsible for all the catastrophic decisions and situations. I destroyed the visions of our future together and killed her beautiful hope in me. I lost the Love I had been waiting for since childhood.

"Moving on" is probably the most heard word these days, especially when I am standing. All these years, I have been dreaming about her and thinking about living with her. But I have never told any of my friends about this, well-wishers and none for that sake.

I have many close friends, but few know I am in Love with a girl. I kept this life of mine personal to me. Sharing everything is not my type of thing. I believe less in people and more in keeping things secret. I am scared of a million items.

But this situation I am in right now cannot be faced alone. I need to speak to someone. I need someone to fill the void that has been created around me. For the past week, I could not sleep, I could not eat properly, and I could not focus on anything. If this continues, then life will become miserable for me.

All this time, I open my social networking page and chat with my close friends about something to divert my thoughts, but I cannot keep talking with them all day. Everyone has their own life and priorities, and at the least, without knowing that I am in pain, why will I spare a long time for myself? I always used to find myself stuck in her thoughts sometimes, and at that particular time, I felt lost.

So now I have decided that I have to speak up. Keeping all this grief inside me is not suitable for long. So I have to come open. The first person I decided to share is a friend from my college with whom I studied for four years. He is the one with whom I am so close and shared everything in college. Maybe he is the one with whom I first openly spoke about the relationship between my Love and me.

I immediately called him and spoke about my Love and my situation in which I am grieving. He understood my situation and tried to make me feel better. At the least, he is the one who never failed to understand me at all times.

I felt better for a while when I shared my grief. So I started this and started to speak about another friend from college. I chatted with him regularly and spoke with him about everything about her and how much I loved her for all these years.

He felt terrible for me and tried to make me think. I felt better sharing my situation with all of them. He immediately shared his own story to make me feel better. He tried to tell me all the possible ways to get involved in different things and move on in my life. I felt better I felt good.

Whenever I share with someone, I feel I am not alone and have many close ones. I felt lost when I was in grief. But when I started to share with others and get out of the pain I was hiding inside my heart, I felt better, at least for some time.

Soon after I realized that I could never have her, I did not cry. I don't know, but I want to continue living with this pain for the rest of my life. The pain is a result of my foolishness and may be one of the biggest blunders I have committed in my life.

I want this pain to remind me of the worst decision I have taken in my life, which affected my life and completely changed my Love's life. She believed me so much that she used to believe whatever I said. And what I did in return was to ignore her. I made decisions that were motivated by the outside world. If I had thought for a moment, life might have been entirely different at this point.

But I cannot stay in those mistakes forever, whatever happened in the past. I am sure I will not come out of this very particular situation ultimately, but I should not remain to do anything. I have to move on, which is why I will keep trying.

But the PAIN caused by my Foolish mistakes will have to stay with me for this life.

II
Purity

It was around when I was in my 7th standard and a memorable part of my school life. I am an introvert and will speak only with those with whom I am very close and comfortable. I don't know if a child at that age is called an introvert, but I speak less and am easily bullied by anyone if their intention is that.

But a sensitive heart of mine believed so profoundly in friendship and love. So I had my boundaries drawn, my close friends identified, and They knew my passion. So I felt love for a girl, and the world is very calm when I keep looking at and talking to her.

She is not someone to whom I am attracted just by her beauty. Instead, her action, behaviour, and everything grab my attention, and I can't stay away from my feelings for her. But then, those feelings made me experience an adrenaline rush. I still remember her smile, her voice, and her look.

"Minute feelings at that tender age got imprinted on my heart, which made me feel elated, like those

feelings are what I needed for the rest of my life.""

This continued for a year, and I never told anyone about my love for her. I never even shared my passion with my closest friends. I never believed anyone and never shared my personal stories with anyone. I felt unsafe with the people around me and restricted everything to myself. I just kept all the feelings inside my heart.

These feelings grew daily, and I felt the same every time I saw her. Of course, I am exaggerating a little, but my feelings made me happy those days.

I was an intellectual guy then, and she was that perfect homely girl, at least from the looks. I never spoke with her freely and never knew her thoroughly. But I know that I like her. And am living my school days between studying, getting marks, and making myself happy by looking at her smile daily. This used to be my daily routine.

Everything was going on as usual when I was in school on a typical day. Everything is perfect in ideal school life. But, in the afternoon one day, I and some of my friends are sitting outside the classroom chit-chatting. And the remaining all are inside the class. Suddenly I needed something from the course, so I woke and started to move toward the class.

When I entered the class, she came from the opposite side. We were about to hit each other, but we did not. we both were in shock. But for me, the feeling is different. I was confused. This was the first time I had come so close to her. So close that I could feel her breath because of the sudden shock.

""Her eyes were looking into my eyes in shock, me feeling her breath, each of us being so close – I can

still remember that moment like it happened today.""

That day that encounter with her became the most memorable in my life. I still remember that day, and my heart rejoices. Although, of course, I am a completely changed man now. I am no longer a child now who looks the things differently. But that moment, how I felt about the encounter on that day, remained with me till now.

I never asked or tried to ask her about that incident, not even after I became close. I don't know why I didn't ask her about that incident. I thought that no one would remember a minor incident like that. At most am just an ordinary person to her, just like any other boy in the class.

But I remembered that moment because she was not like the other girls for me. She is unique, and every moment I had with her stayed in my heart like it was engraved in my mind—a memory that might stay with me till my last breath.

During our school days, one day per week, we were allowed to wear ordinary dresses as we liked. I used to wait to see my girl in a new dress on that day. I want to see her in a dress different from the usual school dress. She looks perfect and beautiful in all the dresses she used to wear.

Not that I didn't like her in her school uniform dress. But I feel so good seeing her in a beautiful dress or gown. I enjoyed her beauty or something like I admired her beauty.

I used to have a blue dress which I got for my birthday. My mom brought that dress. And she used to have a blue colour gown. She used to wear it most frequently. So during those days, it gives me immense joy when my dress colour matches hers. It was one of those little things we children used to have.

If we remember our childhood, we believed in many such things and became happy for all such small tiny things. And life used to be so beautiful in those little things called memories. But now, the world looks so complex when items become significant.

So to make my dress colour match hers, I often tried to wear that same blue dress. I never want to take a chance to miss the opportunity to cut colour-matching dresses with her. Though she used to model other green-coloured clothing in which she looked so pretty, I don't have a green-coloured dress. So the only colour I tried to match with her was a blue dress. That dress became my favourite dress during my childhood. And I still remember these two dresses she used to wear those days and how pretty she used to look those days. Those days even a simple match of colour with her gave me immense joy. The entire day used to be happy and exciting.

This is the way my childhood has been going on for some time. But there comes the hard part. One fine day, she suddenly left the school. I don't know where she went and have no idea why she had to leave. I keep hearing from her friends that she went to study in another school and joined a hostel. I am happy that she has gone to a better school. But she has left me. I suddenly had this feeling that she won't remember me any longer. She will have new friends and people in life, and in that new journey, she will leave and forget me like a regular friend sometime in history.

She never knew that I loved her. I don't know if she had a feeling for me. The story stopped in the middle. Something is felt incomplete. I don't know what to do. I have no option but to wait and see things happening as usual. My tiny heart of mine couldn't take that moment of losing someone looking at whose smile all my past school life went by.

I thought I knew her house. But to be exact, I never knew her house correctly; I know a home where I saw her sometime back and assumed it was her home. Though I had a quick and easy way to my home, I used to take another path that passed through her house just with the hope that I could see her. I wanted to see her more than ever. But, unfortunately, the days are giving, and I feel she has gone forever every day.

Even on Sundays, I took my bicycle and went around passing by her home. But I never found her. I sometimes used to find her sister, but her appearance for me seemed impossible to me.

I made the hard decision to wait for her. Whatever it may take, I decided to wait until it was time to meet her again. I hope that I'll meet her in the future again. And I must be completely prepared. If I came in front of her by god's grace, I would have to be in a position where I could tell her my feeling and well positioned to get her acceptance.

I decided to study hard. I decided to reach good heights in my life, and when it's time, I will try my best to return to her.

During my school days, I used to have this blind belief that whenever I felt terrible, I just closed my eyes and remembered her smile off her and immediately got the required motivation. I have to meet her and be in a good position for her to accept me.

Those days, we believe that if you study hard and earn money, you will achieve everything. So as told by everyone, I used to study to get a good job and make good money.

But now I feel something different. After being a good student and spending most of my time studying and studying, I feel terrible that I have wasted my entire childhood believing in the voice of society and left the tiny pleasure of childhood time.

She is not my age girl, and she is not even supposed to be in my class, at the least. She is my junior. We were never supposed to meet, and I was never supposed to fall for her. But this is what the plan of god looks like. One single act will affect many people's lives in the coming days.

It was my first day of 6th standard. School started after a long summer vacation, and as usual, we are excited to move into new classes. So we became one more step senior. After a few days of school, one fine day, a new girl came to my class. I don't know who she is, and I never met her. But later, I learned from my friends that she was from our school only for many years but our junior.

She skipped her 5th class and directly came to the 6th class after completing the 4th class. Institute gave this option to some well-performing students in our school, and they can do so if the parents want their children to complete their education early.

Now I treated her just like any other girl in my class; I mean, I never spoke to any of my class girls closely. We used to have a thin border between boys and girls all around us in everything we did. Though this border vanished with time, it was strong during my childhood.

Now, whenever I see her, I find some beauty in her smile, and I used to feel that smile was unique.

As my friends could easily bully me, all my friends used to tease me with the name of that particular girl. I don't know why they knocked me with that girl, but inside I used to enjoy those, and outside I used to show like I hated what they were doing.

This continued for the entire year, and in the process, I developed some feelings for her. I become possessive in the process. I used to hate when she asked someone else for notebooks or some other help and used to ask myself, why am I not there in that position of helping her? I wanted to be her primary choice in everything.

I also used to ask her only if I needed anything. No one knows I have feelings for her, and I don't want anyone to know. But I continued to look at her from afar.

As time passed, we entered the next standard, and with this, my feelings also became stronger and stronger.

I expect nothing from her, and I want myself to be the primary choice for her in anything. I don't know what I have towards her, but I am blindly doing what I feel to do.

That was the age when we didn't even know the difference between a friend and a lover; that was the age it was challenging to understand the difference between attraction and love. We find things that make us happy, feeling which make us glad.

That was the age when the only thing we used to do was follow our parents' instructions at home and teachers' instructions at school. Overthinking about anything is not of any significance. That was not the age for realization.

There was no complete view of how the future will be. We used to live in dreams, mostly made-up stories from fantasies we heard from people around us, especially from people so close. But it is not the age to find the real difference between fantasies and absolute truth.

A time when caste has nothing to do with us but will eventually enter into play as time passes. A time when friendship is believed to be the saviour of our lives, and true friends are all who stay around us. A time when it is straightforward for people to cheat and to get cheated.

And most importantly, that was not the age when I could understand the fundamental rules of society. I don't even know that we must follow certain things. And we, how much we try, cannot go against those historic draconian rules.

I am at that age, used to be at peaks when it comes to the feeling of insecurity—never used to share anything with anyone, keeping everything so secret, including my sense. However, one of my friends is somewhat mature in comparison to me. He used to tell me that he liked one of the girls in our school. He is sure about the feelings he has for her. He shared his story and feelings with me, but I had no strength to open up and share my feelings.

I am in a school where the teachers are from another state and are new to the local language and culture. They used to stay in institute-provided accommodation, and their only duty was to educate the children, and they used to spend maximum time with us daily. At times teachers become so close to the students, like family.

We had a class teacher who was so kind and shared everything with us. We are so close to that, ma'am, that we still remember her after all these years. In those days, we used to speak and tell her everything, and about anything, we needed guidance.

My friend shared her feelings for this girl, and that ma'am used to guide us about those feelings like this is not the age, but if you are sure about it, then there is nothing wrong.

When my love left the school with no information to anyone, that ma'am felt very bad. She is so close to all of us, and when one of her students left the school without intimation, she became angry. She became unhappy with her behaviour of leaving suddenly.

But I cannot tell the ma'am that I like her and don't feel wrong about the sudden disappearance behaviour. I thought for some time, what had she done? She maintained a perfect demeanour in school. Every one of the teachers thought of her as very calm and sincere. And this sudden disappearance from school changed everyone's view of that girl, and the only one who still doesn't hate her is me.

But I also want to speak with the ma'am about my feelings for her and ask her opinion. For example, when all my friends were teasing me with that girl, ma'am often approached me and asked me, "Your friends are teasing you with that girl's name. Do you have feelings for her, or are they just joking and making fun?"

I wanted to become open at that time, but I couldn't. I failed to open up my feelings and share them with ma'am. I know I had no strength, but inside, I should have spoken and shared with everyone somewhere deep. Now I know the importance of opening up to people about your feelings.

> *"You must know what to keep for yourself and what to open with your friends and family."*

It is always wise that a single yes or no will be enough. But we fail many times to explain the situation and become open. This will create a good platform for us in the long run. Realizing the difference between keeping secrets and becoming open is an important lesson that is taught in life.

Out of all of this, my love for her has only increased with time, and I enjoy my dreams with her. One thing is for sure my love is pure, and I'll keep it pure by waiting for her as long as I can.

III

Life Moves On

"Life waits for no one. You, at the least, should not wait to do anything and wait for something or someone. You have to move on with life and try your best to get the things you want that matter."

If you wait for things to happen without doing anything, in the best-case scenario, when you face a situation you are waiting for, you will not be able to achieve it or get it. You regret it.

This thought came to my mind. As I was waiting for her, I kept waiting for her, and at the same time, I moved on with my life. I'll try my best to have the best life, and when the time comes, I have to be a successful person for acceptance by anyone.

After school, I passed the exams but with a meagre score. That was the year when the board announced a new grading system, and in that system, everyone around my locality got excellent results. And I stood with awful results in the middle of everyone who was supposed to have gotten better results. I was at my low. I couldn'tcouldn't figure out anything and couldn'tcouldn't lift my head with shame.

I was disappointed. I was very much worried. I don'tdon't know where Everything went wrong. I can understand why this thing happened. I am scared to face people. I am afraid to go in front of my friends around my house and people around my face and answer them when they ask for my results.

People are interested in others' lives when they have too many problems. I come under this category and understand why this tendency has been so imprinted on our minds that until we know the details of our neighbour'sneighbour's friend and other close ones known to us, we cannot stay calm and satisfied.

Maybe we are so jealous of others that we want to hear that they have underperformed, and sometimes we feel for them and want to know that they have excelled. Whatever the reason, it is always true that we are so interested in other mothers' lives than ours.

Believe it or not, the world around us is interested in other people's lives rather than their lives. It cannot be seen from the wrong side. Maybe their intention is they want other people to excel, or they may be jealous of other people. Whatever may be the reason, it is of most interest to us.

So that was the worst phase of my life. Nevertheless, despite all the hard work, I kept up in these exams, and in the end, I did not find the result I got to be satisfactorily equal. But there is nothing that I can do. I can only accept fate and development and movement.

In the middle of this, I have to select a better college for my education. Everyone is moving the best that is available. I wanted to pursue Medicine and become a good doctor. But the typical south Indian family never allows children to make their own choices. Instead, they listen to what society tells them, and the words of the community guide my family's wishes.

My relatives became the kingmaker in deciding on my education stream. When I informed my decision to choose Medicine, the comments that I received were that it was not a good decision and was not a worthy option to explore. And as already quoted, we listen to society more than ourselves and our families.

So similar to any typical family, my family also has pleased that I have chosen Engineering. The stream is supposed to have many career options, as quoted by society, but in reality, this stream is not so different in difficulty from the other stream.

So my dream to become a doctor has vanished. Doors to that desire are closed practically. There is always an option if you have the will. In my situation, you cannot make extraordinary decisions. And at the least, you cannot take any risks. You have just followed the crowd and been like everyone in the society is moving. And no one has taken the option of Medicine. By default, I am not supposed to take that stream of Engineering as it is believed to be risky if society says so.

I sometimes feel that is why it is supposed to be like this. Why, in the first place, create great aspirations in the mind of children and, in the end, make them follow the crowd giving no importance to their ambitions?

Engineering is not my chosen path. I dreamed right from my childhood of becoming a doctor. Every elder around me encouraged me to dream big and become a successful doctor. But those are the same people who forced me to take engineering. Engineering was thrown onto my neck by the illiterate and so-called mature people in society who thinks of themselves as making the most rational decision ignoring the fact that the basic idea of following the decision made by them for me is irrational.

But every time in all these times, my decision changed, my paths changed, and my dreams changed, But the love for her and the feeling I have for her never changed. It only grew daily, and my waiting seemed worthy day by day. I used to dream about her. I used to dream about life together with her. I used to dream about the possibility of meeting her and only felt happy each time.

In the middle of all the confusion that is going on in my life, the only thing I am sure of is about her, and I have never had this high level of clarity on anything.

I moved to the hostel, and it was another phase where I never wanted to stay long. This is the first time I am staying away from my family, and people around me have told me that it will be better; it will be for your good, and I will have a lot of learning from there. I believed all of them. And we only find that society was never sure of these things but only got from others, and they are passed from one to another for generations.

My hostel life started like any other. The first day seemed exciting as you were about to get new exposure. I felt excited. I made new friends. I had my things to manage in the hostel. I have my bed, my separate items, and Everything of my own, and I have to take care of Everything on my own from now. Until now, I have been so dependent on my parents and grew dependent. And this time, I must lead an independent life.

One day passed, two days passed, and a week passed. And slowly, I realized the pain of staying away from home. I always want to enjoy the hostel life, but this new feeling of loneliness and being away from close ones makes me feel void. Alone Lonely

Some of my friends I met in the hostel, unable to cope with the feeling of staying away from their parents, tried to escape from the hostel, and they even left the college. Unfortunately, this has happened to many who converted themselves from hostel life to regular students from home to classes called day scholars.

I am also unable to face the situation. Added to these are the worst administrators who treat us not as human beings but as robots who are supposed only to study and nothing else.

This might be normal for many in the hostel right from childhood, But I pity them. They had their entire childhood in a situation like this. What about all the fun we used to have between home and school? What about the different experiences these people have missed on their journey to get better marks and education? Are they going to regret all these at some point in time? Maybe or not. But for me, I am happy that I had one beautiful childhood, and this hostel life is only temporary for me.

When the parents send their children to the hostel, they are not creating a better life for them, but they are just deleting the beautiful life of their kids between home and school. Their kids might excel in their education and get a promising future and job. But once they grow up, they get into the world with their busy life between family, employment, and career. And in the middle, they will never have a pleasant experience, may never enjoy life, and May never know the true meaning of living a life. Childhood is when you are supposed to bang millions of experiences and have a life. But, once you grow up, society will not spare you, and you will become a pawn racing in this world between career, family, and life.

People are creating a new meaning for LIFE and earning money and earning money. But, unfortunately, the real meaning of living life has lost itself somewhere, fighting society, and the world may never find it back.

But I felt delighted that I was not thrown into such a situation by my parents, and I had a wonderful childhood with many memories to cherish. But, unfortunately, these children have no option. I have seen children crying hard but thrown forcibly into hostels by their parents. They can do anything.

During the times I spent there, I was like a bird whose wings were broken, broken by society, broken by the people around me. How much I try to heal myself, it will be difficult for me to fly away from that place. So now, the only possible way for me is to give away my freedom.

Though I often thought about leaving this place and studying from home, something stopped me. Society believes that only people who stay in the hostel will get good marks. Only those who can adapt to hostel life can face anything in life.

> "*I became a pawn in the game of life and believed that if I stayed in a hostel, I would study better and get better results.*"

So, I decided to stay and sustain there for the rest of the time, whatever may happen. I made my mind and heart believe that Everything would be all right.

I am scared. I am afraid of society; I am terrified of the rumours people will speak around me if I come out of the hostel unable to stay there. That was not the age to ignore the words about me. That was not the age to understand the importance of life over rumours.

And the worst is that my family and friends cannot stop spreading the news about my inability to sustain life.

All the time I stayed there, I had only two motivations my family and her. First, my family is happy that I am sustaining there and studying well. Second, I think about her whenever I am free. I get myself into her dreams of her.

I think about how she will be now. It's been almost 4 to 5 years since I have not known about her and what she will be doing. Will she be doing engineering like me? Or she is doing Medicine. Or is she doing something else? One of my friends told me she might be doing Medicine. I felt terrific. She has taken an option I cannot accept, and I have made a choice. Though later, I realized that society has not even spared her, and engineering is what was thrown onto her neck.

I still remember the symbol of love that I marked on the bench of my college, where I kept her name and my name inside the heart. It might still be there, or someone might remove it. But that moment stayed in my heart till now. At that time, staying in her dreams is my friend to forget loneliness and motivation.

In some ways, I stayed in a hostel and sustained there, and as expected, I came out with exceptional results.

And everyone gave credibility to the hostel life, college, and society's decision to make me choose the stream. Still, in addition to all these things, she also played an essential role in giving me constant motivation. Though she was not physically present with me or talking, the hope of meeting her gave me a mental push.

And with the results, I have been admitted to a prestigious college, one of the top colleges in India. But the college and branch are not what I liked and hoped for. So though everyone around is happy with the result, I am not for what I expected is something more than this. And as usual, I was in depression, worrying about the outcome.

But as usual, I convinced myself to move on and try my best with what I got.

I entered college with a lot of aspirations and hopes. The college is known for creating noticeable alums. Like anyone else, I joined with many hopes for the future.

So I entered college with a lot of dreams and to achieve something. I am a hostel student. Though my relatives forced me to become a day scholar, as their home is nearby and I could stay there and go to college, I refused and applied for a hostel. I wanted to spend time in the hostel and have the feeling of hostel life. I never wanted to stay in my relative'srelative's home, which tried to enter my mind while I was making the crucial decision of my life like they joined our family decision and made me choose engineering over Medicine. Most importantly, I hated staying in someone's home for a long time, and that too for four years.

So I have to choose my roommate as we are given a double sharing room for all the first years. I met one of my known friends who also got a seat in the same college. So we both decided that we take the same room. Thus my long journey of Undergraduate life started.

I met many friends, and I am finding people around the country. There are people from different parts of the country, from east to west and north to south. I want to make friends with many of them, but most are so restricted that they become close to only those who know Hindi. And my speaking skills in the Hindi language are awful, and I used to feel uncomfortable speaking in that language. But I decided that I had to learn this very soon.

After a few days, I learned a lot of things. The life I have been living is just everyday routine life, and many things are happening around the world. However, this college indeed has something that motivates people to do something special.

I wanted to study hard and get excellent marks. But it took no time before I realized that thinking of getting marks and actual implementation to get marks are two far edges of a long stick. If you want to excel, you have to give your best; I failed to share mine. Before I started to enjoy my achievement of getting into a prestigious college, I was forced to get the book in my hand and study, and I failed to do that. And I forgot to do that for the whole four years. I was in the mood to spend my life of 4 years living an actual life with all my friends of mine.

I was soon attracted by the different things the college offers. I got attracted by the unlimited internet provided to all the students and the freedom the college gives. No questions asked, whatever you do. Everything made me feel high in college.

The freedom I have been given all at once made me unrestricted and boundless. I was attracted to fun and enjoying the time. A study has become a secondary option, and just doing time pass with lots of fun has become the primary option.

Out of all this, one thing was constantly on my mind. I waited for her and to meet her with all my capabilities. I should be in a better position when I meet her. So even though I couldn'tcouldn't able to be the topper of the batch, I got some decent scores above the class average. So I used to maintain that and try to be as satisfied as possible.

I all these things that are happening in my life wanted to share with her. So I tried to tell her that I was studying so and so things. And want to hear what she is doing. Everything I wanted to share with her and hear the same from her. But these things are not yet possible. So I did not do a single something to get back to her.

I searched for her all over social networking and with other friends but found no trace of contacting her. So I do not know how to get in touch with her. But there is no way.

I have been moving on with my studies and college life. Everything is going on as usual, with nothing notable.

All these years, Everything in my life changed. Who was I at the time she left to whom I am present? There are a lot of things that changed. What I dreamed of becoming and what I am becoming now. I dreamed and what is becoming a reality. But one thing I did not want to change was the feelings toward her in my life.

Whatever my feelings towards her, Weather it is an attraction or a love or a friendship, I just wanted to clarify it to her. I am just waiting for the moment I can get in touch with her.

IV

Rejoining

I was scrolling the news feed of my Social networking account, looking at random videos, and clicking the like button. I was in the 2nd year of my under graduation degree. I have no tensions that I can speak of then. The only thing we are scared of is the day before the exam. The night before the exam is a marathon for engineers in most engineering colleges.

When I was scrolling through the news, suddenly, a message popped up. It was from a long-forgotten school friend(not the one I liked). When I saw the message popping up, It just blew in mind about the days of my school. One thing that I remember immediately whenever I remember my school day is the look and smile of my girl. How beautiful she is and how much I fell for her.

I immediately opened the message and replied to her.

She: "Hi, How are you."

Me: "hi, I Am fine. How are you".

Starting from these two messages, the conversation discussed our education, what we were doing, and more. After that, we kept on chatting for some time. We even discussed how we have not been in touch for a long time. We also asked about all the friends she is in contact with, and I am in contact with.

I just asked her to let us create a group with all our school friends. She said she had all the girls' contact, and I told I'llI'll add all the boys I am in touch with. But she paused and said she needed to ask others for permission to add to the group.

I expected this. The girls are not ready to always come out publicly. But, on the other hand, that makes it easy to share their contact numbers with others immediately. So I said okay. Let me know if there is a consensus to create a group.

Immediately after some time, she created a group with all the contacts of female school friends and added me to ask all the male friends. She asked me to add all the connections I have to the group. So I added all the contacts to the group.

Thus began our group with all my friends from my school time. A place where each one of us can stay in contact with other friends. It is always said that school friends are the ones who will remain with you for a long. We had the same feeling at that time.

Though I wanted to stay in touch with all my school friends, I was never in touch with all my friends. I always restricted my circle of friends, and only a few were present inside the circle. So stayed in touch with only a few male friends and nothing more than that. So my primary intention behind accepting the idea of creating the group with all my friends is to get the contact number of one particular person, and I am excited to get one step closer to her finally.

It'sIt's been years since I have not heard from her, and I never tried harder to meet her. She is so hidden somewhere to finally meet me in this group. This group will become the founding point for what happens next in our lives. If we did not create this group, I might not have found her for a long time, and my life would have been entirely different from what it is now.

All the doubts I have all these days, such as Where she is, what she is doing, and everything else I can ask her. I wanted to talk to her. Maybe she completely forgot me; perhaps she Is with someone else or chasing her dreams. But I wanted to get in touch with her.

I don'tdon't know about the feeling I had at that particular time. But I still remember how I felt. A sense of achieving something and getting something you have been trying for a long time. So here it ends my wait for all these years for a single chance to get in touch with her. I am so excited that I am about to get her mobile number and have an opportunity to talk to her.

During these very few seconds, millions of thoughts go through my mind. I had never felt so much tension and was never confused to that extent. I wasn'twasn't sure what I wanted to get from this group I just planned and created.

After a few minutes, everyone started messaging the group sharing the whereabouts of everyone. So we are all back in touch. But I just opened the group members tab and searched for her profile.

Yeah... I found it. I found her profile, and I can see her profile picture. I felt so much joy, and I could not express my emotions. My heart just fell for her again after seeing her profile image. It was like everything that I felt during the school days started to feel again.

It was like I fell for her again, wholly new. The feeling I had for her had never vanished, and I could feel my excitement joyfully at that moment. But the fear that is also just beside the happy moments reminds me of the scary fact that she might have just forgotten me or been busy with someone else in her life.

I wanted to talk to her. I just wanted to message her personally. But what will she think if I create a group message for her? What would she think if I message her personally instead of messaging in the group?

All these thoughts are going on in my mind. But what made me happy is that I have her number now. I saved her number with her sweet name. So my contact list looks complete, with her name added to the list. It is so exciting that we all used to speak about everything everyone is doing in their life. It just brings back the wonderful old-school days.

The night went by, and the next coming days went by. The group used to be active as usual as every new group. Whenever someone was free, used to message in the group, the conversation continued by others who were free. This went on for days. But one thing that was on my mind was to message her personally and ask her some of the things I wanted to ask her.

A few days passed, and I decided to message her one day. I took the decision and sent her a personal message, and after a few seconds, she replied. I was awestruck by that reply. Getting an immediate response from girls is not normal, and I got that, so I am even more excited now.

But my hands were very cautious in messaging her. I was never so attentive in chatting or messaging someone. But with her, I don't want to feel uncomfortable by messaging something that is not supposed to be asked. I don'tdon't even like to send a message with many typo errors.

I asked what she had been doing all these days. We just chatted for some time, and I was surprised to see that a few boys from the group had already messaged her on the day We created the group. I got angry at my friends at that time as they messaged the person I admire the most, and I took all these days with fear in my mind.

I asked myself why I was late. When I have waited all these years to get in touch with her, why did I not message her the moment I got her number? Maybe I am scared. I am scared that she might think badly about me, and perhaps I am afraid that she might ignore my message because we are already chatting in the group. Maybe a lot of other reasons, but I have messaged her at least now.

One thing is evident to me. She is very typical of me as she is of any other person. There is nothing special about me. But for me, she is more special than any other person. How can I tell her directly that she is the only one I am chatting with personally and not with any other female friend from school? Even though there are friends with whom I have studied even more time than I studied with her. Still, I am more close to her than any other person.

She left me long back, and even after she left, I stayed in the same school for the rest of my primary education. Of course, I was with all my female friends and many others during this period, but no one could replace the place she had occupied in my heart.

So I am finally talking with her, or to be precise, I am chatting with her. And now I feel glad that all my wait has finally reached here.

There is a very famous saying. If you have a genuine will, everything around the world will help you get those things, either directly or indirectly. The quote correctly suited my situation. I never tried anything to get in touch with her. At least as hard as I am supposed to. But I just kept hoping to meet her by some means, and everything started from that single message I received from an old school friend on that particular day.

Now I never asked any of my friends for her number. I know they must have her number, but asking is way too far, and everyone might feel wrong about my intentions. At least, this is what is taught to us by society that asking the number of a female is, by default, a malicious intention.

I was, at the least, not the initiator of this group creation. That day if that particular friend from school had not messaged me, I don'tdon't know what I would have done to get in touch with her. I should have kept waiting all my life. Or should I have tried something eventually, unable to wait even longer, or should I have taken it for granted that I am not meeting her and maybe moved on with my life?

But one thing is for sure: life might have been entirely different for both of us if it was not for that group.

Now my day has one more routine that is added by default when I started chatting with her. I am messaging her about the happenings of my life and the essential things I should share with her. This has become a routine. Everything is going as usual.

We both share things, and we even discuss our other friends. She even used to share with me, who are all the other friends of my batch who were chatting with her, but she promised me that she won'twon't tell anyone I was talking with her. So that made me feel that I was something special to her.

Whatever her intention may be, I have taken the word in the way I wanted to hear it from her. We even used to discuss the messages each of their friends used to send her.

I used to be on the lousy side sometimes. Whenever I felt that someone was becoming close to her, I used to bitch about the other person. I am not like telling lies, but the absolute truth about that person. Sometimes the truth is the thing that is enough to make people feel wrong about a particular person.

I felt I was doing everything just for my love, and my intention was never bad about anything. I just wanted her to treat me as unique more than anyone else, and no one should come in between us both.

She used to tell me that she won'twon't even talk to her other female friends in the way she chats with me. This single sentence is enough to take me to heights. I felt so special to her. It made me think that I am getting even closer to her, and she is treating me more and closer with time.

We understand each other mother's lives and each other past lives as we have not been in touch for a long time and have shared many things and incidents of life.

We are moving forward as we are both there for each other and have no one else in between us. Everyone else is only after us.

She is doing engineering at a college that is near my college. As I said, I am studying in some reputed college, and she always treated me like an educated guy. But I know I am much changed from the type of person I was in my school days.

I am happy that her home is near me, her college is close to me, and now she is also near me sharing everything with me. I even used to share the details about my family's happenings, and she told me about her family's details.

This may be what I have waited for all these years. The moment may have finally arrived. The moment to finally get closer to her and find out why I feel so special about her.

I have completed different levels of education without seeing her for many years. Now during this journey, I have come across many girls. Even in the attending college where I am studying, I have many friends who are so beautiful that many of my male friends try for them. But I had never felt anyone so special the way I felt for her. I don'tdon't know why but the truth is that whenever I think about a girl in my life, I just used to think about her and used to dream about how she might be and what she might be doing.

This may be what will happen when your heart is filled with someone such that there is no space for anyone else to occupy. However, we also know that things that occur during childhood are difficult to forget. Because of that, my childhood attraction is not that easy to give away.

Whatever the reason, now I have all the chances to get closer and discover our relationship and what I want from this.

Suppose she is that one person who we finally go on to call life partner. Or is it just the childhood attraction that kept me waiting, and there is no way forward between us as we both are wholly changed people from what we used to be in school? Or maybe I just wanted to know about her because she has been left uninformed to anyone.

Whatever the reason, I wanted to make it clear and move on with life-based on that decision. So I started to know more about her. And the same way, she began to understand more about me. She used to chat very freely with me, and I used to do the same.

But none of us is moving forward from the border of friendship. This is because we are so close in terms of company and not in a situation to move forward and take it to the next step. Or at least we have never thought of any action above us that we can take if possible.

Everything is going fine between us, and we don't want to spoil this. But, on the other hand, we don't want to expect something better and eventually damage the present. So we are both very comfortable with our present unnamed relationship and are moving forward with this unspecified relationship.

Whatever the future holds, we are so happy in the comfort of each other. We are slowly getting so comfortable in the company of each other, and we never tried the thought of naming the relations that is present between us. We know that we are happy in it and don'tdon't want to take the step to call it and, in the way, destroy the essential relationships between us. This is because we are so scared to take action.

V

Propose Her

We have been chatting for some time now. We understood what others were like and discussed the most personal things. We slowly and slowly become close to each other.

Initially, I was very scared to talk and cautious before sending or asking anything. But now I feel very comfortable asking anything and everything and telling her anything.

She also used to share everything and anything. We used to chat for hours and share most of the things happening in our life with each other.

Now I do not know how this is moving forward. I don't know what the name of the relationship between us will be. And I never thought so deeply about it. But one thing is for sure. I am very happy because I have been living in her dreams all these years, and finally, here she is, speaking with me the same way I wanted her to speak with me.

One fine day everything was normally going, and she messaged me in the middle of something. I felt something was wrong, but I do not know why. I immediately replied to her.

She chats with me normally, but I can feel strongly that something is not good with her. So, I insisted she tell me what is going on.

Then she, with a lot of hesitation, said that she was getting a lot of stomach pain and could not bear it. I did not know what to say to her because I never cared about anyone so much when someone told me they were not feeling well.

I can feel the tension inside me, and not sure why I am feeling like I am getting pain. I asked her for the details and tried to make her feel good. I tried to ask her about her friends and asked her to go to the hospital, take the tablets if needed and rest.

I wanted to visit her personally, but I could not because even though we are close enough to share everything, meeting a girl is felt bad by the society around us. If a boy goes to meet a girl and if they tell it as a friendship to society, then society will start creating rumours around us.

And on top of all, the shyness that I have in asking her whether I should come is what stopped me from going to her and taking care of her. Even this is what my mind and heart agreed that I have to go to her right now.

And the worst is she never wanted me to come, which is what I understood from her words. She used to say that she was very scared and that what if someone found out she was chatting personally with me? I don't know what the big deal in it. But for her, this is a major one, and she tries to keep it a secret. Maybe no one knows the problem, but society taught us that a girl should not talk to a boy unless it is most required.

She is so scared that the people around her will question her about the talk she is having with me. A girl is never supposed to talk to a boy, and when someone finds such close talks between a boy and a girl, it will be in no time a big rumoured topic of the society, and she is scared to face such a situation.

Though I could not reach her personally, I tried whatever suggestion I could give and tried to be with her virtually until she felt better. She went to rest, said goodbye to her, and asked her to message me about her situation and how she was feeling as soon as she woke up.

But this situation has made me think about something I have not been able to find out for a long time. All these days, we used to hide our chat. We used to chat as if we didn't want the rest of the world to know about us.

And we never tried to ask ourselves what each of us will be to the other person. A friend or more than a friend. All these days, we are in a relationship which makes us feel comfortable. So we never tried to name it. We never thought about much to name this relationship. We are so comfortable that we don't want to try to name it and spoil the present relations ship.

But now it's time that we have to take it a step further and name it. Only when we know what we are for each other can we behave as we are supposed to.

I am sure that this relationship is more than friendship. I know that I love her and will do anything for her. But I don't know whether she feels the same for me. But now it's time to find us. Now, if I have to know the relationship between us, I should have acted accordingly to her when she said I am not feeling well.

If it is love, I should have immediately, without any thought, reached out to her and taken steps to make her feel good. But now I am scared that if I meet her, society will take the step of naming the relationship. I don't want society to name this and hence have not taken the option to visit her.

But now I have to decide and tell everyone what she is for me, and I want to treat her how I want to.

But here comes the scary part. I am very much confused about how she felt about me. She now treats me more than any other friend she has. But is this enough to ask her to love me? Is this enough to take it for granted that she loves me? Maybe or not.

But I have to ask her; that is the only way to find out. So I decided to find the right moment and find it out.

Days have passed, and I am scared every day to ask her. I typed the message many times and clicked on backspace for fear of damaging the relationship. This continued for some days.

One day at night, I was chatting with her, and she was sharing all about her day. And suddenly, she told me, "I want to ask you something."

I was confused because she had never asked like this before. Deep inside my heart, I feel that this is what I expect from her. But I am not sure.

I said, "What is it? Just ask me."

Then she waited to reply for some time, and I am waiting

She: "Nothing. There is nothing. I asked."

Me: "you said you want to ask something. Why are you scared to ask me."

She "there is nothing. I just said to see how you react."

Me "No, there is something you are hiding. Please tell me what it is."

She "I wanted to ask did you had dinner."

Me "Don't make me a fool. Please ask what you want to ask"

She is diverting the matter and not asking for something strong. But deep inside, I feel something. I feel she is trying to tell those magical words. Maybe I am expecting more, but

I am feeling that. So I am decided to bring those things from her to know for sure.

I kept on asking her for a long time. But she kept on saying the same thing, that there was nothing. But I have not stopped. I kept ignoring her messages, saying I'd only reply if she told me what she wanted to say.

After some chat, she agreed to tell, and then she took some time and again the same process. She again started to tell me there was nothing. Now I got irritated but had to make her say. I am trying all the ways to get her to tell those things she is not telling. But she is strong even.

The more she resists, the more I feel she is about to tell those magical words I wanted her to tell.

But here comes the story-diverting thing. While chatting, I unknowingly told her.

Me "I know what you want to say. So don't worry, tell me."

Now she caught hold of these words I told and started to ask me what I thought I wanted to tell. But I cannot tell her because If I tell her and those are not what she planned to ask, I might eventually be damaging the relationship. So I am strong not to tell even.

Now the story turned two into a side blame game. She used to ask what I thought, and I used to ask what she wanted to ask. This continued until midnight, but none of us was opening the conversation forward. The same thing is going on and on.

But in the middle of this, she said she was sleepy and wanted to sleep. She wants to escape from the situation and divert the conversation. And she said if I don't tell her what I think, she won't reply to my messages from the morning.

I became the victim in the game between us now. Now she is playing with me with that one line I said. But now I am supposed to tell you what I think. So I told her I'd tell her the next day and asked her to sleep.

Now I didn't sleep but started thinking about all the conversations we had and what she was hiding from me. Is it that she wanted to propose to me but was scared, or is there nothing but I am just making the situation favourable for me?

But this is the chance I have to take and ask her what I wanted to tell them for many days now. So that midnight, around 1 AM, I started typing what I felt about her.

> *""Dear love, I don't know how you react after seeing this message, but I have wanted to tell you this for a long time. If you don't feel the same way I feel for you, please don't damage this relationship with me. I cannot afford to lose you, and I will be broken down if you completely put me away after."*

> *"I have never felt so close to anyone as I feel with you. I never shared the details that I shared with you. You are very special to me; you listen to whatever I tell you and share whatever you want. You are my human diary, and you are my other half. I LOVE YOU."*

I sent this message and slept. I just slept into her dreams, hoping she would see the message in the morning and tell me her opinion. I am scared because all the wait for her for the past few years now comes to this final proposal, and the future of our relationship depends on how she reacts to my proposal in the early morning.

I am thinking of multiple things in my mind right at that moment. Did I hurry in proposing to her? Should I have taken more time to understand more and then proposed? Does she have any feelings towards me, or am I just a normal friend with whom she felt comfortable sharing things? Am I using the situation and taking advantage of the freedom she has given me?

Freedom is a scary thing. When a person is left uncontrolled with no restrictions or boundaries, felt, then they do unaccepted things. She has never restricted how I should be with her. She made me feel comfortable sharing anything I felt about. So I even decided to propose to her.

Now, as I have sent the message already, I don't want to take back anything and wait for the sunrise so that she reacts to the proposal.

The morning is very important to me. All my wait for years had reached a situation of naming my feelings towards her and how she felt for me. And this day is special in my life and both of our lives.

I went to sleep, but the night was not that tense. I felt relieved that I had said the words I had kept with me for days. I felt bad when I could not understand the relationship between us. Now with this, I'll get an idea of what we are meant to each other. I have told my thing, and now it's her turn to reveal what she thinks.

It was early morning, and as soon as I woke up, I opened my mobile and saw the chat for any replies. I found that she had already read the message but had not replied to anything. I felt scared and confused.

What might she have thought about the message?

Did she feel bad that I had taken advantage of the situation?

I felt bad for myself and continued to scold myself for the action. Now I eagerly need a reply from her, and I don't want to end this relationship with her abruptly. I am so used to her that now I cannot afford to lose her completely.

Thinking about all this, I was preparing to go to my college. I wanted to know when she would message back to me. Million different things are going on in my mind. I am not scared. I felt better and relieved as I confessed my love. Now the decision is in her hand. But I feel scared about losing her completely. I am scared to face a moment in life without her sharing everything and scared that she will have a very bad impression of me for taking advantage of the situation.

Millions of things are going on in my mind; I can feel it. I started my walk towards my class. That way, I passed by, and though it has been two years, I feel very different. I felt something new around me.

I am in my class and no mood for anything. I looked at my mobile for a notification, a message from her. In the middle of the day, she messaged me. She was chatting with me like I told nothing to her last night, or she didn't even see my message.

I was confused for a moment. Did she read the message? Then suddenly she started to ask about my message last night.

She asked, "what is that message? I didn't expect such a message from you."

Me: "Okay, I wanted to tell my feelings to you. If you have no feelings for me, no issues, let's be friends.

She: "No, after you have confessed, it will be difficult for me to be your friend."

Me: "what happened now, don't spoil the relationship that we had between us. We can be good friends."

She: "How can you tell like that? It will be difficult for me to be your friend after you confess your love for me."

This went on for a moment. I felt scared and thought that the worst was coming. She seemed didn't feel good about my message. But I am sure that I did correct it by confessing my feelings.

I left for my room, and she said she would message me later.

I was in the thought of different things. What would happen if she no longer wanted to talk to me? What should I tell her to forget about my confession? Can I at least tell you that?

I understood that it would be difficult for her to continue the friendship if she had no feelings for me. But I had a feeling that it won't be that difficult. She can at least treat me like a normal friend she had.

I am confused; if she doesn't have feelings for me, why do I want to continue our relationship? What I want from her. I thought for a long. But not sure of anything. Maybe I don't want to lose sight of her. Or I hope she will surely get feelings towards me in the future.

Time went by, and in the evening, she messaged me again. We started to speak normally. She is as normal as she is daily. I thought things would be back to normal. But in the middle, she keeps saying, "I cannot forget what you messaged; I have been thinking about it the whole day."

Me: "There is nothing to think about if you have no feelings; I just respect your feelings."

She: "How can I not think about it? What you said is not something that I can easily forget."

Me: "Yeah, I agree, but the more you think, the more I am scared that our relation will damage."

She is confused. Sometimes she talks about something else, and suddenly she brings back the matter of my proposal, talks about it for some time and then goes back to another normal chat.

Anyhow the talk between us is going on. She suddenly asked, "Can I tell you something."

ME: "yeah, tell. What is it."

She: "I am scared to ask you."

Me: "Why are you scared? Just tell it out."

She: "I LV U"

I was awestruck by looking at those messages. I didn't expect this message when she said I want to ask you something.

Me: "Love you too," I said back. "Why are you scared to tell this."

I have achieved something in this life. For a moment, I was on top of clouds. She finally confessed.

I have been in love with her since childhood, and I was never sure that such a moment would come. You will sometimes know when a moment comes, and this is the moment that will change my life ahead. I had that feeling. Now all these days are something, and her confession will change my path for good.

Yay, she finally confessed, and all my wait for all the life I had till now has finally reached here. We will be in love and will lead a life together from now. Now I proudly tell the world that she is the one, she is my girl, and I am hers.

VI
New Relations New Problems

I felt a new life when she accepted my love and confessed her love for me. Something good is coming my way. You can sense that feeling when you have waited for something so long, and finally, it arrives. The moment is here for me.

We kept chatting that day. When she proposed to me back, my mind immediately went on to ask her about many things. Though I know a lot about her, Now I have a new kind of relationship with her; I want to understand her more and more and become even closer to her.

Now the boundary I drew around me with the people seems to start vanishing. She is inside my boundary, and I can share everything with her, and there is nothing I can hide from her.

Soon after, she asked me about my caste. I was completely confused. Because all these days, I believe that we belong to the same community. I was completely mistaken. She is from a different caste, and people in our society are against such relationships between people of different castes.

But as an educated person and she is more attracted to me, nothing can stop us from becoming one and spending the rest of our life together.

I was confused when she said that society wouldn't accept us both. What was society to do with anything between us? I was scared for a moment. Is there anything that is going wrong here?

Should we enquire about the person's caste before we fell for her? Is that the first in the process of finding a life partner? I started to think about both of us spending a life together, but she was certain that the families would fight against us and that we had to be strong with our decision.

There is nothing that can stop us both. But why was all this not taught to us in all these years? Why do family and society teach all the morality stuff without ever letting us know the true reality of society?

> "*Morality, from the view of society, is a completely different thing. The boundaries we draw around us in the name of morality, truth, and good vs. bad are all created for our own sake and will change based on whether society is comfortable with them for the time being.*"

We are becoming close and close as time passes. Before, we were in the circle of friendship and the relation of close friends. But now we are in an even closer circle. This circle has nothing in between us to hide. We started to understand each other. We begin to share everything, and in this process, we start to move into a situation where the other person is a must for survival.

We don't know where our path will lead us together. At every point in time, we are very sure in our hearts and minds that society will come against us, and we should be in a situation to fight against all the odds.

Now, everything seemed achievable. My relationship with her is worth a fight, and I should be ready to fight. But the biggest problem for both of us will be our families.

In the end, all families, including ours both, are part of that same society that has rules on which persons are allowed for a particular person. These rules won't allow any intercaste relations. Though we live daily with people from multiple castes, when it comes to creating a relationship with the family of other castes, some things make us take a backstep. The force is so strong that it existed throughout history across a large part of the country and is still present in many places.

No one knows when these will change, but we have decided that we should not be the victims of these rules. We should convince our parents and everyone and accurately happen everything as planned, a life of us together.

I know the words are simple to be spoken, but the reality will be known when we face the situation. But I have decided one thing, and I should be in a comfortable position that there should not be any reason they can raise her to reject me by her family. For that, the most important thing anyone sees in another person is a good Job. At least I have been told right from childhood that getting a good job is an important part of life and is a great achievement.

I have to get a proper job and be comfortable asking her family to accept our love. I am sure I'll get a job in college, but I have to get the best available job.

These are on one side going in my mind daily. Even she might be thinking millions of things about our future together.

We started to think about each other in everything we did. We are first to share something with the other person whenever something happens. This makes us feel happy and comfortable. Even if there is any problem that we are facing, sharing it between us will make us feel easy.

Those days daily nights, we used to talk for hours, a regular part of every love story. Daily we used to chat whenever we were free, another regular part of every story. But I used to get dreams about her and me now and then, and it only kept a smile on my face in the morning when I remembered them.

I wanted her at any cost. I even discussed with my cousin's sister the possibility of accepting love marriages in our homes. My cousin's sister was somewhat close to me those days, but I damaged the relationship because of misunderstandings between our families. In those days, I used to talk to her frequently, and on one such occasion, the topic of love marriage came up in some way. I wanted to ask her about this thing. Though I wanted to tell my cousin's sister about my girl, I was scared. It is too early to share with everyone, but I will share when it comes.

The topic came when she just played with me and asked how many girlfriends I had. Using that conversation, I told her, "how can I have one because our families won't accept inter-caste, and if I want to find one from our caste, I need to ask the girl what your caste is before proposing, which is the worst situation awkward thing that can happen."

I told this intentionally to see how she would respond to inter-caste. To increase my hopes, she said, "Why Our family at present may not accept, but you can convince, and with time passing, inter-caste becomes normal, and before you reach the suitable age, they will be in a situation to accept.

These words from my cousin seemed so good to me. My fight will not be as tough as I expect. I just thought if I was overthinking the situation that my family is strictly against inter-caste or her family. Our families may be mature enough to think and accept us. Maybe my girl is overthinking and is scared too much of a small problem. It may be time that will change everything.

These words from my cousin had been in my mind for a long time. My hopes of being together with my love are getting stronger and stronger. All is going well, and there is nothing that will stop us.

As usual, I share everything with her. I even share this chat with my cousin and sister, my love. She didn't respond positively. I can sense that she is not convinced that our parents will accept us so easily. Though she is not saying anything, I can feel that there is something in her mind that she is so scared of.

I insisted she tell, and she started to speak.

"It will be very difficult to convince our families. At least my family because I know my family, and I am very sure they won't accept our relationship. I don't know what will happen, but the probability of us getting together will be more tilted towards a not-possible thing. But believe me, we will fight till the last, and we will try our best."

I am confused for a second. I have been thinking about it all these days and getting scared. It is just now that because of my cousin's words, I felt a little calm. But the words she said made me afraid of what will happen. I don't know why she was so scared. I asked her why she was telling me like that.

"See, I have an incident in my family that made me conclude that the fight with my family will be a tough one. My aunt loves someone, and she is in such deep love that she doesn't want to marry anyone else. So she said the same in her family, but the guy is from a different caste. So the family, as expected, rejected it. So the girl tried to elope with the guy, but the family forced her to marry someone else. This has not happened for very long.

There is also another incident in our family. One of my relatives has fallen in love with a girl, and he wants to marry her, whatever may happen. He conveyed the same to his family, and his family rejected him. He has tried hard to convince the family, but all his efforts are in vain. He used different ways, and in the end, his family started to search for a girl to marry him soon.

Unable to share life with someone else, he went out and married the girl he loved secretly and brought her home. His family did not accept that. They can do nothing but keep him away from family things. Still, he feels alone even with a large family. He is not invited to anything, and no one greets him; he comes to everything just with the hope that everyone will accept what he did at some point in time. But nothing has happened for years now.

After all these incidents in my family, I am scared about the fight that we will fight and the choices we have to make in the future.

She made me confused and scared. I felt like listening to horror and a sad story mixed. How can such things happen in real life? All these are supposed to be films and stories. But in real life, their own family turns against the love of children, giving importance to societal rules more than their own children's wishes. I don't get the logic in all these. I don't know what to speak to her. I was quiet for some time.

All of a sudden, silence occupied the place between us. She said what she could, and now it's my turn, but I am completely confused. How should I respond to it?

I told her, then what is the way ahead. What is that I can do to make her family accept me? I told her that I was ready to do anything to get her in my life and share my life with her.

She said, "*First, let me tell you. You first make sure you can make your parents agree, And if you are sure, then come and talk to my parents. Don't worry much, and I am just telling you that the future will be with tough decisions, and whatever happens, we will fight. Don't think bad and think that whatever happens, we will be together in this life.*"

The last sentence she said seemed so perfect. But the first lines attracted most of my attention and thought. I can't get those things on my mind and make myself comfortable and hopeful.

Do I know how my family will react to this? All this day, I am sure that I will be in a better position to convince my family, and it is only her family that I need to convince. But now I started to think If I thought wrongly about my family. What if even my family is completely against such relations? Maybe we never had such an incident in our family, which is why I don't know about my family's decisions in such matters.

But from the way she spoke, she was sure that even my family would be against accepting her, and she even pressed that convincing my family would be the toughest part than convincing her family.

Now, this is getting over my head. I couldn't find a place in my head to capture all these things in my mind and think about these complex things. I am so nervous that even gathering data, she tells me, becomes difficult. She said you don't think much, but I have to think; it is our life for whatever sake. I am in such deep love with her that I can't imagine someone else occupying that place. I expect she is in the same place and how she is facing all these thoughts. For a moment, I felt immature, and she was well-grown and completely aware of societal things.

As she said, I told her that, whatever happens, we will fight. I don't want to show my fear of losing her and make her feel bad. I told her we would fight the situation and be together.

Now, after the talk, I couldn't think of anything else. After all these things that I am aware of, how can I, suddenly?

Everything became so wrong for me. The world seemed so cruel at that moment. I want to fight against all of these.

But, the fact is, I am not new to this situation. This has happened several times and will keep happening for some more time. I often heard the love story of my friends or relatives; I heard the sad end and how the families were against them, and they got separated and moved on with their lives.

Whenever I hear this, I used to feel that they didn't fight well and I won't be in their situation, and I am very well placed to make things right and convince everyone. But now I am in the same position as everyone, in a situation to think about society.

The time and stories happen as they are supposed to happen every time. And whenever you feel that you are the one who is supposed to change the way things are happening, you will move to reach a situation where you find yourself locked up in the same routine old story. The sad part and the sad end you never expected in the beginning and hoped to face.

True, there are stories where they fought against all and came together. But at what cost, Do your family still speak to you as before, Are you still invited to all the things that happen in your family, Is your love accepted by your parents that they should not see your partner with anger? If any of these aren't happening, I won't consider it a success.

You were getting your love at the cost of making her lose her family, not providing a family for her, and making her have no one other than you is not a good life you can give her.

In the journey to get life together with your partner, you are missing a family, and your partner is missing a family. Maybe you both are together, but you are not together with both of your families.

These are multiple things that are coming to my mind. When she told me about her family, she made it clear that whatever happens has to happen with the agreement of both families. She cannot sacrifice her relationship with her family to make a life with me. She doesn't want to make herself away from her family to have a life with me. And this is justifiable. Overall she has no father, and her mother is everything. Her mother cannot sustain her elder daughter to go against her wishes.

She even had a small sister, and if my love did anything against the family's wishes, the family would behave harshly toward her small sister and show anger toward her. She didn't want any of these things to happen. And hence she is very clear on her part that she will be within in the fight till we convince both families, and we will continue our fight until they agree without any side thought of doing anything secretly. Thinking about all this, I went into a deep sleep.

> "Just that now complex things are turning into. I am locked up in a complex puzzle. I find no way out but to face the situation. I am ready to face and fight, just

that I am not ready to face the consequence."

In reality, when someone tries to run away from a fight or anything, it is not always to be taken for granted that they are scared to fight or face the situation. It is not always true. They are not scared to fight and not to run away because of their incapacity to fight; it is just that they are scared of the consequences afterwards. They are scared to face those aftermath consequences.

VII

First Visit

Our relationship is growing stronger and stronger, and we can already feel a sense of togetherness.

For many days we have been in love, and I always wanted to meet her personally.

I can't even remember the last time I saw her. Some days back, when I was walking outside my granny's house, I was thinking of something and roaming in front of the house. I suddenly saw someone passing by from the side of the house, and I didn't see the face of the person, but I was sure it was a familiar person, and the only person whose home was to that side was my girl.

I wanted to rush to the side of the house and see if it was her. Before I decide and rush there, she is already gone.

I still remember that day, and I got stuck there feeling somewhat sad and depressed. I don't know, but I felt like I am missing something. Something very close to me, and I know I wanted something in life.

Though I always wanted to ask her about meeting personally and talking, I never asked her. I don't know, but except that I proposed first, she is the first to ask everything else. She excepts me to ask, but I am shy enough to escape those first steps.

One day in normal conversation, she asked when we could meet personally. I feel happy because she asked for a meeting personally. That is the thing I couldn't be able to ask for. I immediately responded to her to meet them personally.

But we need a place to meet. We never wanted anyone else to know about our relationship, and we don't even want any problems from our family, friends, or relatives now.

She said she would meet her small sister on Sunday in her hostel. Her small sister is staying in a hostel close to her college and frequently goes there. She asked me to come with her this time. She always used to go with her friends, but this time she asked me to come so we could walk and talk as much as we wanted. I accepted that, and we decided that we would meet the next day evening at the decided place.

It was midnight, and I already felt the night was very long. I couldn't wait to meet her. It's been years since I have seen her directly. I still remember the smile on her face, the childish looks, and her long hair of her. And whenever I remember her, I only remember her childhood face in her green dress and the cute smile on her face. Now I will be able to see her face after all these years.

The feeling of meeting her personally after all these years instilled a sense of achievement. I couldn't believe that everything was happening as I always wanted them to. Those moments are of great importance in my life.

There is something weird I feel this time. I was in my room, where I had been staying for the past few months, but I had never felt so awkward in the room. I want to go out.

Go out and wait for the night to disappear, the sun to rise, and the birds to wake up singing in the trees. Everything that used to happen every day, but today I wanted all those to happen for me so fast.

I came out of the room and sat on the bench in front of the hostel. I sat there looking at the deep sky, counting the stars, but my thought was elsewhere. I was thinking about what I should speak about when I finally met her, what I should talk with her about for such a long time. Will she like me after looking at me directly? Will she find me comfortable, as I have always been an introvert? Should I take something with me, a flower or something that makes her feel good? I am never so romantic.

This moment is so new. The feeling I was in seemed so good to me. I want to stay in my dreams all night, thinking about her, looking at the sky. I can feel the cold night, calm nature, and the dark sky, but the feel of the dreams I was in is remembered forever.

I came back to the room and slept only with the hope of waking up for the day to meet her finally.

It was the day finally, and I was all set and went to her college. I was never so tensed and felt awkward. I was eagerly waiting for her to come out. Holding my mobile in my hand, I can feel my legs, unable to stay strong.

I called her and informed her about the place I was in. I do not know which one is her hostel. She asked me to wait in front of a Shop, and I was waiting there, looking around to escape the awkward look I might give when I finally met her.

I don't want to create a bad impression after meeting her. I want to make this meeting memorable and make her like me. I want her to feel comfortable with me. But nothing else is in my mind other than my fear and confusion.

She called me and told me to look to the right side. I know she asked me because she is there. I am a little scared after all these years of meeting her. she is here. She was walking towards me. I was completely astonished after looking at her. I cannot feel the world outside of me. She wears blue jeans and a red shirt, which suits her well. It was a black pouch purse in her hand, and her long hair looked the same as many years before. I for a moment felt the world stop for a moment.

There she is, my girl, looking like an angel in my eyes and a perfect one for me. She looked the same as she used to look during childhood. Nothing changed, just that she is a little bit older than she used to be in school.

As I started walking, she signalled me to come and get into the auto.

I immediately started moving towards her and got in the auto. We started moving to her sister's college, and on the way, I was completely down and nervous. I was not sure where to start the conversation. Only one thing was completely stuck in my mind. What is her opinion of me, as this is the first time she has seen me? But I cannot dare to ask her. Surprisingly, she started the conversation, and we started talking before we reached where we had to get down. We got down and started walking towards her sister's school, which is a few km away. We planned to talk about the school.

We both started walking, standing far from each other. I couldn't go near her. Her sister's school is outside the city, and the way is empty, with no houses or people. Now I understood why she decided to go there because there would be no one on the way, and we could speak as much as we wanted to on our way.

Though I was very scared, I started to speak something. Everything unrelated. I want the conversation to continue and don't want her to feel the awkward silence between us. So I kept speaking something.

But on our way, though we started walking and speaking, I was standing somewhat distance from her. I never went so close to her. It's not like I don't want to go close here; I am just afraid of everything happening there. I am very careful of every word I speak and every action. I am never so careful and want this visit to be the best.

While walking, we encountered a few people moving opposite our way. It was a deserted way with no houses nearby, and I was not sure where all these people were coming from.

Whenever someone is coming on our way, I notice that she becomes calm and silent, and I can sense the fear in the scared look she gives towards those passing people. I assumed she was a little bit scared of people and didn't want any trouble from her parents or friends.

I tried to ask her why she was so scared of all the unknown people passing by. She just gave me a look towards me with a cute smile. That smile got my attention. It was like I fell all over again for that smile.

We finally reached the hostel, and she asked me to wait outside. She doesn't want her sister to see me. She asked me multiple times if I wanted to visit her sister. But I know she is scared that if her sister knows it will be a problem, so I said I would wait there and asked her to visit and come back.

She asked multiple times about what I'll do alone and do. I didn't want to come. Finally, after some time, she went inside to meet her sister, and I was waiting at some distance from the hostel. It was a deserted road, and there was nothing I could do.

I can only stand there doing nothing. I can't find at least something to sit on. So I was walking to and fro on the road doing nothing. Just saw something on my mobile.

Now I feel comfortable with her. After our long walk and talk, finally, I was comfortable. I was looking at the mobile, and whenever some unknown person walked that way, I tried not to give an awkward look. I just tried to act like I was waiting for someone.

I started to hate waiting there and doing nothing whenever some unknown person gives an awkward look towards me. And I know it is only a few minutes before she goes inside, and she might take a long time. But to my surprise, she came so soon out of college. I can see her coming out from the gate and towards me. I don't know why she can so fast.

She came, and we started to walk back. I asked her why she came very fast. She again gives that smile I can keep looking at for so long. She said nothing but a smile.

We, on our way back, started talking about something and walking. But as we came halfway, she suddenly came close and held my hand. I was completely surprised. I wanted to take that step, go close to her, and hold her, but I couldn't. But I didn't want to give her an awkward look when she did. So I hold her hand, and we are so close.

I feel her so close to me. I had never held any girl's hand so close and felt so happy. I can feel my heart cherishing that moment and being happy about that move.

She is holding my hand and smiling with her head leaning on my shoulder and walking the way on a road that is almost deserted. There is nothing so perfect as this for the first visit to my love.

I was holding my love's hand with her head leaning on my shoulder, mee looking at her cute smile and walking silently on the deserted road with silence occupying us, the moment that just remained in our hearts forever.

But whenever she noticed someone coming toward us, she used to leave my hand and move far from me. I could sense the fear in her, and as soon as they left, she used to come back and hold my hand back.

Before we realize we have come to the end of the road. I don't want to end this so fast. I am so happy about this meeting and walking the road to school and back. But I couldn't find a way to spend more time with her. She then suddenly said shall we go back for another walk.

I was surprised again. She smiles when she asks and looks at me. I don't know, but I like all of this. Her face, I just wanted her to come in front of me, standing there smiling as I kept looking at her smile forever.

So we started our way again back towards her sister's hostel. We are not going to the hostel again, but we wanted to spend more time together, and this is the best way to keep walking and talking with no one around.

She walked holding my hand, and I, too, went so close to her. I felt like I was with a close one and had someone special in my hand. Today, this moment for sure will stay in my heart forever. Not the thing that she held my hand specifically, but the feeling inside me that I never before had. This may make you do anything for the person you love.

That feeling I had when she held my hand is so strong that I keep feeling the responsibility for her happiness. I felt like I had to do anything to keep that smile on her face, and whatever happened, it was to be ensured that the smile would stay forever as long as I was there.

I am very happy on that particular day, and so does she. I can sense the happiness in her smile and eyes after meeting me after all these days. I always waited for her right from my childhood when she left school without intimating anyone and all these years of wait brought her to me, and we are in this particular moment enjoying togetherness.

A long walk on an empty road with a person you love the most and the first experience of being close to someone you have loved for years. The moments in impossible to recreate whatever it takes.

So we went back to talking so much. Our second walk towards the school and back was comfortable for us as we both started to let go of the shyness we used to have in the first few minutes of the meeting.

Now we both are comfortable, and this is what we wanted to achieve with each other. To make ourselves comfortable with the other and share everything with the other person.

We came back, and it was already late in the evening. It's time for her to return to the hostel, and we both don't want to end this meeting abruptly. We both need to spend more time. But there is no place I know, or she knows where we can go.

We cannot go walking the same way again as it is dark, and walking on such a deserted unknown road is not safe, and I don't want to take such a risk with her in the first meet.

She even wanted to spend more time with me. When I said, will you leave back to the hostel? Couldn't she answer? What else can a girl say to show her willingness to spend more time?

I wanted to find a way to spend some more time with her. But as usual, I failed to find a way. She suddenly, with a lot of unwillingness to ask, told me we should keep walking instead of taking an auto to my hostel.

I was shocked that it was such a long way, and I couldn't get such an idea to spend time with her. But the idea was beautiful because we could walk all the way talking about everything we wanted to and stay together some more time. With no thought, I said YES.

I feel happy that she found a way to spend more time with me, and I am excited that I can now spend some more time with her, holding her hand in my hand and walking to her college.

That was the longest walk I had ever made in my life. Twice to her sister's school and the long way to her hostel. I never imagined such a long walk would feel so good.

And I was shocked because she walked such a long distance. I thought that she could walk such a long distance when she asked me if we should walk to her hostel. But I didn't ask that question because it may sound like I didn't particularly appreciate walking, and I don't want to create doubt about whether I like walking. But on our way, I asked her multiple time if it was okay for her to walk such a long time. Tell me we will take an auto if you don't feel good on the way. But she was such a wonderful person she walked to her hostel a long distance with no complaint.

We both reached the hostel, and she didn't want any of her friends who might roam in front of the hostel to see me with her. So she went to the hostel, and I started my way back to college and took an auto.

But the day with her was a memorable Feeling. I call this a feeling rather than a moment because I still remember how I felt that day, and it is the best feeling I had ever experienced before and only made me love her more.

VIII
Faith

We started meeting multiple times. She found a garden far from her and my college but a beautiful place to meet where we could sit and talk and stay together for as much time as we wanted.

We started meeting multiple times, and whenever we met, we just visited the garden in the evening and sat there talking as much as we wanted to and leaving. We started to spend more time together. This is the only place we used to meet because outside, as we stay close to our homes, there is a chance that our parents or relatives may see us together, and we don't want to face those situations at this point.

We decided to meet again today, and I am getting ready to go and meet her. We planned to visit the temple nearby and take god's blessings. I want to pray that whatever happens in my life, please don't take away the girl from my life.

I took the auto and went to where we regularly met. I reached and waited for her to come. I messaged her, and she was already on her way.

I always wanted to go to her college, wait for her, pick her up, and travel together. But she never agrees. She always wanted to come and visit me here because she was scared that someone would see us together and create a problem.

She is so tensed and worried about her surroundings all the time. And as I was thinking all this, she came getting out of the auto.

Her dress is golden and red in colour Dupatta, a perfect combination of a person I love and the colour I admire, her long hair and the smile on her face, I still remember the smile she used to give whenever she saw me. That makes my day. That smile is what I want in my life forever.

The smile on her face may make me so fond of meeting her regularly. I am more in love with her smile in special.

We started our walk together toward the temple and started talking. She maintains some distance from me while we are walking on the road. She is so conscious of her surroundings that someone might see us together.

Even though I used to fear that someone close to us might see us together, I used to hide my fear.

"You look beautiful as always," I said with love-filled in my eyes.

She just smiled with no reply.

"What if someone like your friends sees us together here," I said, playing with her

"Will someone come this way," she said and left my hand, seeing someone coming from a distance.

"what happened," I said. I don't want her to leave my hand

"Who is that walking towards us? It looks like one of my friends," she said with a scared voice.

"No, it was someone and for sure not your friend," I said, putting my hand over her.

She again laughed and came close to me, holding my hand. We kept walking towards the temple. I always wanted to go to the temple with her and tell god that this was the girl I wanted in my life, and don't plan for anyone other than this.

We reached the temple, and she started to tense again, looking at the crowd. She started rushing towards the temple with a lot of fear.

"Don't worry; no one will see us here."

"come fast, and let us go inside first."

We went inside and started praying the god. I just closed my eyes and started wishing to make life easy for all my family and her.

"Please show your kindness to my family and ensure a good career for me. You have done everything good for me: a good college, a good family. Now I have come here with someone special in my life. I came to ask you to make this girl stay with me for this life. I love her more than anything, and I cannot ask you for anything more than her in my life. I will visit you many more times with her if you make our parents agree to our marriage." I prayed to god with a lot of faith in him that she would stay with me forever.

"Whatever you have planned for me, I hope she is there in that plan and will be in my life with me, and if she is not, please make a new plan with her staying with me forever.

She immediately took the Kumkum and kept it on my head.

I also took it and kept it on her forehead; at that moment, that particular second, I felt togetherness.

In Our culture, a boy is not supposed to keep Kumkum on a girl's forehead unless the girl is his wife or to-be.

When I kept the Kumkum on her face, she looked at me closely and smiled. I know the reason behind her smile. I know the smile meant a lot, conveying acceptance of our bond, indicating that we are now together and supposed to be before ever.

A smile was telling me that I am all your's. A smile that speaks to me takes in your hand and travels together forever. A smile that, for the first time, spoke a million different things.

My heart just became so light in that particular second and moment, and I could sense the happiness inside me. I felt she was all mine and hers, and no one could ever separate us.

I held her hand, and we both started to look into each other eyes. There is nothing that can recreate the moment, then.

Inside the holy place, with her hand in my hand, her eyes looking into my eyes, telling me we are supposed to be together forever. What can we not give to make this reality? What can we not do to live a life together?

I just turned towards the god and said

"This moment, I wish to stay forever with both of us. Whatever may happen in my life, make this girl stay with me. I can ask nothing more than this from you".

I held her hand and prayed to God one more time to make this moment stay with us and our bond as strong as our faith in god.

We just went aside and sat in the temple for some time, she sat close to me, holding my hand, and the feeling of us together there that evening was like we were already living life together. Our souls are already together.

Love is not just sharing what each other is doing or not just making each other happy by giving the gifts they want. Love is to make each other feel complete and make each other feel a sense of life togetherness. I felt that feeling that evening, and we promised we would be together for the rest of life.

We left the temple, went back to the garden, and sat there for some time. We made some love with each other and moved to our respective hostels when it was time.

The day was not like a normal visit. Though I felt very joyful after meeting her, I had a different feeling that day. I can sense it deep inside me and the thoughts that I am getting on my way back to the hostel.

That day visiting the temple had just brought like new attractions in me. It was just magical how we both stood in front of god and conveyed our wishes to stay together forever and make our life as we wished. It was like we had made up our minds and were just a few steps away from leading a life together.

But the moment will always stay with me. It gave me a true sense of love. All these days, my perception of love was completely different, but now I feel about her differently. All these days, I was feeling to make things right to get her in my life. But now I feel like she is already a part of my life, and I can't even imagine her not having me in my life.

That night we talked about the same thing. The feeling we had when we spent our first evening together in the holy temple. She felt the same way I felt but couldn't tell me in person, so she messaged me after reaching the room.

We chatted all night and slept. A memory that will be in my heart forever. In the future, whatever may be the situation, whatever job I do, whatever place I may stay in, whoever may stay in my life, the only thing I cannot imagine that night was life without her. It looks scary to me.

With the thought of us together, I dreamed all night and had a pleasant sleep.

Time had only taught me the importance of hope, I hoped to meet her at some point in my life, and here I am with her. Now I have the same hope that time will take us to a position where we both will lead a happy life.

But I know for sure that there are two sides to the coin of HOPE; one side will increase your hopes and ensure you that everything will be all right, and the other will throw you from the tip of the mountain. I know this, and I only wish everything goes well between our families, and I pray for it daily to god.

IX

KISS

Today I am excited to visit her because she promised me something. She promised that she would give me something that I insisted on her all night while chatting with her.

I got ready, came out of my hostel, went to the chocolate shop, and brought dairy milk—her favourite chocolate. I think the tastes of all girls remain the same everywhere, they are found in chocolates, and they are found in makeup kits. But my girl's makeup kit is of no or little interest, but the chocolate, she will do anything for them. Whenever I ask her what do you want, her reply remains the same, bring chocolates for me.

I brought the chocolate and started going to our meeting spot. I reached the location and messaged her to start. I don't want her to reach the location before me and wait for me. The story is the same always, and it is taken for granted everywhere that boys are the one who is supposed to wait for girls.

But a few days before, during our last meeting, she was the one who kept on waiting for me, and I could see the anger on her face. That is not exactly anger on her face;

that is irritation not because I was late but because of the location. She is worried that someone will see her there and scared that they will get doubt us both.

As I kept waiting, she arrived, and we started walking towards the park and kept talking about the day and our friends.

Me: "What reason did you tell your friends? Did they ask anything else"

She: "I told her I am going to meet my aunt."

Me: "Oh god, you started telling lies to your dear friends; that's too bad, you will get girl children."

She: "What are you talking about."

Me: "There is a belief that if we speak more lies, we will be granted, girl children."

She: "No, I was asking why you are telling me I will get girl children; it is us who will be getting them."

I was shocked at her reply, and she was not thinking about the main content I said, but she couldn't accept it. I started to talk about her separately. She wants me to talk about "us" and not "her." I was happy inside me for a moment, and a smile was visible on my face.

She: "why are you laughing, don't laugh, please. I Am scared someone will see us."

Me: "Why do you always be tense? I am here, dear; if someone sees, we will tell them we are in Love. At some point in time, we have to tell everyone."

As usual, she has not replied. She is just looking around and seeing if someone is there. So we moved fast towards the park and went inside and sat there.

We sat, but none of us started to talk about anything. What can we talk about? We both are typical introverts. Then she suddenly dragged my hand, holding it, and leaned on my shoulder. I held her hand and started to feel the sense of her hand.

Then we talked about something, and we didn't even notice the time, but I was always waiting for that one thing she promised me she would give me. But what can I expect? Is she also scared as me? How can you expect a girl to kiss a boy for the first time when a boy is so scared?

The time has come, the park is about to close, and people started moving. Then suddenly, she came close and kissed my cheeks. That was my first kiss from her, and no other girls other than my parents and sisters ever kissed me.

Then I immediately took her face in my hand and started to kiss her.

That was our first kiss, and we were not connected. Then as time was over, we came out of the park, and on the way, she held my hand and said, "Now I kissed you, now I am feeling like you are all mine; you are all mine."

I was so happy to listen to those words. A girl so scared to speak anything and even talk to me now tells me to my face that I am all hers.

I want to hug her and tell her I love you and am all yours. But as we are in the middle of the road, I cannot do that. So I said to her holding her hand, "I am already completely yours, and you have complete right over me."

She smiled and said, "I am also completely yours; tell me I am yours."

ME: " Yes, my Love, You are all mine, and no one expects me has right over you."

Then we both took separate autos and reached out to hostels. I was thinking back to the room about how close we became in just a short time. I had never imagined I would be in Love, but now I have already started to love someone more than anything. How surprisingly, time is moving.

I reached my room and started to think about the kiss. The kiss we had together for the first time. It was a moment to be captured. The feeling is so new to us. We met many times in the same place, but today the place became so close to me that it is where I had my first kiss from my girlfriend.

I have already started waiting for another meeting with her so that I can take the first step to kiss her. I felt so dumb. It was always a boy who kissed the girls for the first time. But in my case, I asked the girl to take the first step. Yeah, I am so scared to kiss her, but I felt how tense she must be when she thought of kissing me.

We chatted that day all night and went back to sleep, writing another beautiful memory in my mind. This beautiful feeling registered in my mind more than a memory to be remembered.

X
Confusion

I was in my final year, and I wished I could get a good job and a happy life with her. I prepare well for everything, and interviews are just around the corner.

She even wishes the same. We both wanted that if I got a good job, I could convince her parents somewhat easily. But the real problem of caste issues stays.

I started to give multiple exams, and the first few were disastrous and demotivating. But I started to try more companies continuously.

And the day finally arrived. A day of interview for a company, which I was very doubtful about whether to attend or not. Because the job is not what I am interested in, I cannot afford to miss the chance. She even said the same thing try it, and you get it, okay, and if you do not, then I am not interested.

But somewhere deep inside me, I regret attending the interview. Anyways I just attended and waiting for the results. But somewhere, I felt I would get this, and I was a little scared about my choice of this job.

I started to feel, "am I going in the wrong direction? Am I making unwanted decisions".

When the results came, my name was just there, and all my friends were very happy for me, and I even started to smile joyfully, but somewhere inside me, I started to feel a little scared about my choice of this job.

I feel inside somewhere I regret being selected for this job. But now, as I have been selected, I cannot attend any more interviews, and I have no other option but to accept the job.

I informed her about my job to my love, and she is very happy about me. She was happy that I would now have a settled life, and we could try convincing both of our parents.

I just started to accept that I now had to move into this job and convince myself and I got used to the feeling that I got a job and could not apply for another job now.

Now I started to spend more time with her. Now, as the job has come, the biggest challenge in front of me was to convince our parents. But the task is not as easy as it may seem.

I was scared of something about the future—the future of mine, the future of us together.

As I got the job, she started to accept more time to be spent with her and even more time with her. We even started to quarrel multiple times.

We even sometimes stopped talking for a long time, and we all returned to normal soon. Things normally go between a couple of closes—small misunderstandings and moments we can remember.

We met more frequently, and she became so possessive of me. I started to spend full time with her, and my end exams are already here.

I am finally leaving college with a job and a desire to face the challenges I wish to face, which the future holds for me. The moments stood there in my mind.

It was just months before I started my job, and in these final holidays, I was enjoying my time at home and could spend long nights chatting with her. And this was when we had a lot of misunderstandings and a lot of understanding between us. Knowing each other and getting close even more.

But it was also the time I had enough thought about my future. This time has provided me with different thoughts and fears to face in the future. Day by day, we are becoming close to each other and depend on each other.

And it is very clear to me that she cannot live without me. She becomes devasted and confused whenever I forget to talk to her on a particular day. She becomes depressed. Maybe she got used to me so much that I became a necessity in her life.

But that is not all. The worst is yet to come. We were never sure that our family would accept our relationship, and she never wanted to go against her family's decisions.

So what is going on in her mind? She was always very sure that her family won't accept her. At the same time, she is never ready to go against her family's decisions. And the worst situation is that she cannot live without me. It became a little complex for me to think about all this. And provided that I am free enough to avoid such thoughts, I got involved in such deadly horrific thoughts all day.

I love her very much, and all I ever wanted was for her to be happy. I have indeed waited for her since childhood and wanted her in my life. But the future is uncertain, and now with the love I have developed towards her, the only thing I want now is for her to lead a happy life.

One day when I was chatting with her at home, my mom somehow doubted something. She asked with whom I was chatting. I just wanted to tell mom about her, but it is not the right time. And I thought I was not ready to tell my mom about her and face the situation now. It was never the right time for me, and I was never ready to tell. I just realized it was very late.

I told my mom it was my friend, and I avoided talking about my love for my mom. But somehow, she is doubt full about something. She then began talking very seriously.

She started to tell how important societal cultures are and how important that we marry only the person belonging to our caste. I didn't know how to respond and just kept listening to her. I am sure her words are directed at me though she is talking to all of us.

But I just somehow listened and escaped from the situation. How can I tell her I love a girl from a different caste? How can I convince her when even with the slightest doubt, she began giving such lectures?

The mistake was never with her or anyone. It was a society that made them think in that manner. We are just pawns in the old cultural society following the old rules which are unwritten but became so important around us created by someone we were unaware of.

The thought process becomes so imprinted in our daily lives in the manner that we should never think outside our caste or culture, and it is very difficult to change them. Many people have tried different ways to change the ways societies believe these old things. But what we did. We made these people so great that we never followed their teachings, at least in the society where I live.

All these thoughts are going through my mind. I have enough time and space to think about all of these.

Before I met her, I wanted to meet her and possibly get life together with her. But my behaviour changed over the past two years of love with her. Now at any cost, what I want is her happiness. I became a slave to her smile, and I cannot see her face lose those smiles.

Consider the future, when we are about to tell our parents about our love. Now, after listening to the thing that mom has said, I have very sure that they are not going to accept her in my life. They wanted someone badly from our caste. So can I convince them? Can I change their mind and make accept a girl from another caste? I don't know. Because of my family relatives, no one has ever had a love marriage as far as I know, and I can only find it directly by asking them, which I cannot do at this point. At least I don't have the guts to make it clear to my parents at that point.

I asked about her family's situation and the chance that her family would accept our love. I asked her to understand the future we have to face.

She is very well sure about her family that at any cost, they are not going to accept me. I don't know what those mean, because she is deeply in love with me and at the same time, she is very sure that her family will not accept. So what is she about to face? At the least, she is not ready to go against her family for me, which she made clear before.

She wanted her family and me simultaneously and was very sure that her family would not accept me. The situation became so complex for me. I cannot think of anything for some time.

I just asked her, what if our families won't accept and we have to live a separate life? I don't know what happened, but she started crying. She went into depression, and I could not control my fear.

She is such a sensitive person, and I know how she will face the future. I don't know. But the only thing I am worried about now is her smile. Her happiness. I want nothing but for her to live a happy life.

As I said earlier, my behaviour changed completely after I met her. Before I propose to her, I want her in my life. And after being in love with her for these years, I wanted her to be happy with a smile and nothing more than that. But when I knew that the smile would vanish if our parents won't accept, I started to worry a lot.

A girl who had nothing in her life but just a normal life. She faced difficulties that I had never spoken to. She lost her father at 14, and the pain she might have faced is unpredictable.

With her mother taking the responsibility of raising both girl children and my girl before she knows about life, facing the responsibility of taking care of her small sister. The situation is the hardest part of life.

After all these years, she had been living a normal life and now loved me more than anything. And she couldn't afford to lose me. And at the same time, she cannot go against her mother, who had raised them after the death of my girl's father. Her decision to be unable to go against her mother's decision is understandable.

But one thing she is missing is that the puzzle is so complex. She does not realize it and is just happy in the present moment. But it is time that we have to think about it and plan accordingly.

At least I have to do something, and it is my responsibility to take care of her and her happiness. When I promised that she was mine in front of the holy god when we visited the temple when I kept Kumkum on her forehead at that time, I was, by default, entrusted with the responsibility to take care of her and her happiness.

XI

Decision

It was a small misunderstanding that had happened between us. But this time, I was profoundly serious. I was worried if I was the correct person for her, and I was unsure if we would stay happy together. These thoughts are one side besides how we will convince our parents.

Love exists only where one expects nothing but love from the heart with no doubts.

I truly love her, but the doubt I had about the future together is a little sacred. I expect her to understand me, to always be with me even if the mistake is on my side, and to believe anything I say without question. I felt very selfish and foolish, and I started to hate myself.

Out of all this, I made a foolish decision in my mind. I wanted to leave her now rather than create hope for the next few years and finally get separated with different paths because our families won't accept us.

Society had a major role in my decision, and more role is played by my brain, unable to face the future and fight for what I love. I am fooled by the scary face of the caste system and the furious decisions of society.

I accept that this is very foolish and a blunder that I cannot forgive myself for this life, but the only thing I wanted was her happiness. I could not keep myself calm when I started thinking that it was me who started all this love and because of me, she might lose her happiness in future.

Not that I wanted to leave her forever, but I wanted to give her some time and relieve them from this and reduce their hopes in me so that even if both of our parents won't accept, she won't be completely devastated. I want to create a bad picture of myself for this to happen. I wanted to show myself that I was not correct for her. And I don't know how to do that because, in the process, there is a probability that she will be completely devastated and might lose herself.

In the middle of all of these, I am simultaneously worried about my career. In our society, it is very common for parents to force a girl to get married around 22. I know this is a very young age. An Individual has many things to do other than just marrying someone at that age. She will have a lot of dreams in her eyes and plans for her future. But her parents, who encourage her from childhood to dream big and try for something big, force her to accept someone in her life and be a good wife. I don't understand this. If parents are already prepared to crush a girl's dreams and plans, why create hopes first-hand right from childhood?

I once asked her what time her parents could wait to start plans for her marriage. She said that she wouldn't marry till one year after college completion, and only her parents would start plans for her marriage. She is presently in the pre-final year, So I have almost two years to be sure to face the situation.

These two years are very important to me. I have to achieve my career dreams to reach a better position and be comfortable for her parents to accept me.

But these two years will only increase hopes for her. Within the last two years of love, she got used to me so much that she completely depended on me. So I want to make her prepare for whatever might happen in future.

I have made up my mind. I wanted to achieve both my career and my love. I am ready to face my family and go against them, but I don't want to separate her from her mother and sister. Her sister is so close to her that she never likes to leave. So I have to be in a position to be accepted by her family position. The only thing that can make her family members accept me is having a great career. Nothing more than that can help me get her without leaving her family.

So I decided to start preparing for a great career. I have to achieve a better position these two years and return to her to fulfil my promise to speak to her parents about us together.

But one thing is clear: the journey will be so long. The journey takes a long time, and I don't have that time. Now in a few days, I'll be joining the job, and she will be joining her final year of engineering. And after she is done with engineering, she can, at maximum, stop her parents for one year from a marriage proposal. I have to be ready for them. So I have two years to set my future, so I have to face difficult situations and accelerate my growth.

Another hard decision also needs to be made at this point; whatever the future holds for me, I have to make her lead a happy life. So I decided to avoid her for a time so that I could concentrate on my future and, at the same time, let her learn to live without me. Yes, I have made up my mind without thinking more and planned to use the current quarrel between us to avoid her. So I stopped replying to her messages and started to plan my preparation.

The decision is very hard for me to make. I know the decision is not a good one, but as I have loved her with all my heart, I have to do everything I can to make us come together so that we can live happily ever after.

If I now think about my decision, I don't know what made me do that. I loved her so much, and how did I decide to avoid her?

I made a decision and just attached reasons to satisfy myself. No reason I made it is satisfying. I am a fool. I am a person who not only destroyed my life but also destroyed the hopes of a truly loving girl.

From that moment, I stopped replying to her messages. But I couldn't resist. Many times I just wanted to reply, saying to her the entire thing happening within my mind and say sorry to her. But I couldn't. all the days I stayed at home, I felt like I was not doing the right thing. But one thing is that everything is for the good of both of us.

Sometimes I feel like saying, "My love, sorry for everything I did, sorry I decided on our lives without even asking you, sorry that I have planned things with you and expected you to follow the plan without telling you the details of the plan. But believe me, my love, everything I did, each step I took, I always believed that it would only lead to a beautiful life where we both live together for life."

She messaged me thousands of times. She called me many times. Every time I behaved like I was doing such a favour for her. But I never realized how much she was suffering because of my behaviour. She messaged me very frequently, and each time I ignored her.

I just got busy with my new job, life, friends, and challenges. I just felt my life moving on.

But even during all this time, every day, at least for one time, I think about her. I think of her before going to sleep and after waking up in the morning.

But once a decision is made and the time has passed, you must face the consequence. And I am facing the result. I remember her name daily before going to sleep and the first thing after I woke up in the morning. I want to take the phone and call her and tell her I love you. But I cannot.

She messaged, called, and tried to reach me for a few months. Then one day, she just messaged me.

"Are you leaving me"

When I saw that message, a tear started rolling in my eyes. I couldn't control myself. I couldn't feel well, and something was wrong. I felt it and am the reason for all. At that moment, I just wanted to message her 'I Love you."

But I still cannot understand why I didn't reply. I still to present-day ask myself what stopped me from messaging her or answering her call on that day. I still ask, and I fail to answer myself each time and am in the loop to find the reason.

After a few days after that message one day, she just messaged me

"Can you call me last one time"

I didn't respond to this message. In the night, she messaged me back with a long message.

"What happened to you? I didn't expect this from you. You know why I accepted your love the moment you proposed to me. This is because you are not like all, and just after I accepted your love, you started talking about our future together and our marriage. I liked that very much."

"I fell in deep love with you all these years. It's been only three years, and though very less time, it's been like a lifetime of us together. The moments I have with you, the long-distance I walked with you, without ever believing I could walk such a long distance. A girl who used to cry with leg pain when walking for a short distance just went on walking with you for long distances without any pain, looking at your face, seeing your face, listening to your talk. I just fell for all of these. "

"Dear love, I never expected you to be such a weirdo. You made me believe all and, in the end, just dumped me. Do you remember you once said that whatever happens, you will stay with me for this life? What happened to all those promises? Are all the promises made by you wrong?"

"Are all the promises made by you wrong? I can't even believe it. I just like a dream, you know. You have decided to leave on this road alone, forgetting all your promises that you will be with me. Now you have decided to move with your life leaving me here alone."

"I was very happy before you came into my life. I never had anyone in my life. Just my family, my little sister and a few friends. It was going very well for me. Then you entered yourself, created hopes and suddenly made some decision out of the blue and left me. But the person I was before you met and the person I am now is not the same. Before, I was very happy with myself. Now I got used to you that I find it difficult to be happy with myself after depending so much on me."

"Okay, now I even don't want all this. I don't want to follow you when you don't even think and reply to me. Let's stop all this for once and all. I take it for granted that one cheater just cheated me with hopes and moved on. You are an evil dream in my life."

"It is very difficult for me to forget all this of a sudden. It will take some time. But after all, you have decided that you won't need me; I'll also start to tell myself that I am all alone and will take some time to get out of all of these."

"goodbye forever. Please don't ever try to contact me back. And even if I message you back won't reply because I cannot control myself to ask you, telling myself that let me ask one last time. Block my number so I won't be able to contact you back."

She sent such a long message, and I can feel the pain inside her when writing this message.

While reading this message, I couldn't control myself. I just felt bad and foolish about my decision. I cried all night that day. I just went into depression. Ultimately, I am the reason for all that is happening with me and, importantly, her.

But even in that situation, I didn't message her. I didn't take any steps to get back to her. Why did I? What stopped me? Only one answer, I don't know.

She spoke that day's words are still in front of my eyes. I each word she says and the pain inside her words, I feel every day. But the real pain is hers, and the reason is ME.

I don't know what happened in my life. A single and foolish decision of mine just damaged everything. I take that decision alone, or do I have some force that compelled me to make that decision?

I can ask myself millions of questions like these. But what is the use of all these when you have committed a mistake, and now you cannot take back those?

I hope this all is a dream and I have never made any wrong decision to stay away from her. I hope to travel back in time to undo what I did. I want to eliminate all the pain I created in her life.

But all these thoughts are to satisfy me. Ultimately, I am not ready to accept that I am a fool and make her suffer her life. I create a big hope for herself, and while she plans a castle of life plans together, I destroy the castle with one foolish decision.

XII

Realization

I opened my eyes early in the morning, worried, tensed, and scared of the future. The planned future seems to collapse, and nothing works for me now. The only reason I feel right now is losing the one I loved for many years.

When I decided to leave her to chase my career and come back for her, I had only one thing in my mind she would wait for me. I never asked her, and I just took it for granted. I made my mind up on the assumption to satisfy myself without solid reasons. I wanted to satisfy myself, and I did that, but at the cost of losing someone, I loved for years.

I wanted to achieve a better position and failed in that. For the past two years, I have been doing the same boring job with no growth and nothing else—just a routine job that should have been there without any reason.

I felt she was becoming so dependent on me that I wanted to make her forget me. But why? In love, each one is supposed to be dependent on the other. If that is not the case, there is no love. Why did I miss this point at that time?

For these two years, I have had no clue what she is doing and what is happening in her life. I just remembered the smile on her face and her happy life and just lived on these, and with all the new friends and life around me, I just carried on with my life.

Every time I tell myself that, I will go back to her. But I never thought whether she would wait for me. Because after the last message she sent, it is very clear that she is very angry with me. And in such a situation, she has no reason to wait for me. Because I completely ignored her and never replied to her.

Two years passed like a bullet train, and here I am in my home, just thinking about her after all these years. She said, "My family will wait for two years and plan for my marriage."

I remembered that and thought if I loved her, I should not miss her, and the time was passing, and I should reach her. But I have no means of communication to reach her. She deleted her social networking sites, and she deleted her old number. And all these years, I even deleted my social networking sites.

So I reactivated it to see if she was still there. I opened her profile, and we are no longer friends. Because the last time she blocked me, and now she unblocked me when she reactivated her profile.

I just wanted to send a message to her. But there is a lot of fear inside me. I wanted to say sorry to her, but with my mistake and the pain I created for her, I am unsure if she would accept and forgive me.

My handshake to do anything on her profile. So after a lot of thinking that happened for almost 2 to 3 days, just one day opened and sent the friend request.

Yes, I did it and waiting for her response on that. I waited for a day, and there I opened her profile again, and I could see that there was no option to cancel the request or send a request. This happens only when the person you sent the request marked you as spam.

Yes, she marked me as spam. This is acceptable after all the pain I have created and the havoc I made in her life.

So I remembered all that how much she tried when I tried to avoid her. She tried all the ways, head, and tail, to just in touch with me. And I feel I need to do it to make her forgive me.

So I decided to message her. But something stopped me then. Maybe she moved on. Maybe she completely forgot me and didn't want me. I just thought about this for someday, and then one day, I just opened her profile, and I was completely devastated. I lost myself. I felt the world stop for me. I felt as if my life should have ended then.

It is her marriage photos. She just updated her profile with her marriage photos, and someone is tying the knot with her. I can't believe that it is true. I just wanted that everything is a dream. But I cannot always change things in my favour.

I remember all the promises I made, all the wishes I asked God in that holy temple, the promise I made when we met in the park, holding her hand and telling her we were mine when we met for the first time and we tell ourselves that no one is going to separate us. All these things are just reminded in front of me, and here I am, seeing someone who had entered her life and she had already become a life partner for someone.

When I just saw the pics, I felt the importance of her in my life. My life just turned upside down. All these years I took grated that she will wait for me. But I couldn't control my tears when I saw her with someone else. I can't eat and can't sleep.

"With the smile on her face in those pics, I felt this was what I hoped for and what I wanted when I stopped replying to her. Then why on earth can my eyes not control, my heart feels like it's bleeding, and why does my brain feel that I cannot think anything anymore?"

I feel someone is telling me that I am guilty of something. I am the reason for everything that is happening. I might try to escape from the fact, but the real culprit in this story is ME. I made that foolish decision, and it is me who has to be blamed, and I deserve to suffer.

I felt the real pain on those days. For the next few days, life was hell for me. I just wanted the entire universe to end now. I even started to imagine all the possible ways to get back to her.

"But all those are just hypothetical dreams, as usual, to satisfy me, and nothing is going to work, and it is known to my brain. But my heart can't be ready to take the truth. I can't digest the truth."

All these days, right after I woke up and right before I go to sleep, I remember the name and face of the girl, yes it is her I planned for all my life, and now today, I feel I no longer should remember her or should imagine my life with her because now she is married to another man.

Just sitting on the bed and thinking of any possible ways to get her back was what I was doing for the past month, and though you have no limitations on your thoughts, in reality, nothing seems to work.

Everyone at some point feels LOVE, a feeling that needs no introduction. But being loved by someone else is a gift from heaven. What else do you need if someone loves you so much more than themselves? You already got the most valuable thing in this human existence.

You cannot buy love, you cannot force someone to love, and you cannot introduce love to someone. Human is advancing in all ways, they are reaching far distance in different fields, and without a doubt, technology will solve many problems that human beings face. But one thing that no advanced things can do is to get love.

And for me, this realization happened very late. It is so late that the realization will not help me get back the person I lost because of my foolishness.

I have always believed that society is advancing and moving toward change. In no time will all the differences among the people, le whether it be differences in caste or culture, change.

But I even failed to realize that to change these differences, there is a long way to go. Because there are so deeply founded in society that only a revolution is needed to eliminate them.

Today I stand in front of the mirror, look at myself, and start thinking about what can be done. Because it's time that I need to plan something about the future as I cannot stay long crying for the lost one.

So I decided to move forward, try to forget the past, and start a new future with or without love. I opened my mobile to take the first step to delete her photos from my device, but my hand was not supportive. I cannot. I am weak, depressed, and lost. I thought for a moment, let the photos be there but don't open them now and then.

One thing was very clear in my mind. Things are not going to be the same. Things will be so different. But one thing suddenly struck my mind. Things are never the same. Do they? Just throwback to my childhood when am completely a different person. I can't compare myself with that character at that age. Back in my college day, that was another version of me.

Yeah, many versions of me changed with time according to the conditions of society, and it has never struck my mind the changes I have been going through. With time, my attitude changed, my character changed, my interaction with people, and most importantly, the people in my circle changed. But one thing never changed how I missed this one. It is her, she is the one whom I have loved right from my childhood, and I never imagined another one in my life other than her. This has been so long that this change of hers in my life is affecting me and making me things all these days.

But now I have realized that this is the same as another phase in life that will hugely impact life, but life has to move on.

I am sure I cannot get her back in my life, and I have to move on with my life with someone else. The thought was so scary that I started shivering when I thought an unknown person would come into my life.

I became so convenient that I took her for granted in my life. And now she is gone. Nothing makes sense in this life. Everything became so complex and understanding how things work became a separate-scope subject for me.

Having a single thought like, if I am suffering hell right now with the feeling of missing her, how might she have felt when I started to ignore her? I realized how I made life hell for her over the past two years. And her decision to move on with someone else is understandable. Ultimately, she needs someone to move out of the hell I created for her.

Now it's time I understand the consequences of my foolish decision and accept things. There has to be some way to unite back together. But this will only make things more complex, and with all these things in my mind, I just started to move on in my life.

But the journey is going to be hell for me. I have no one to share with. I have to suffer my own; at the very least, I deserve all this, for I am the reason for how things are going in my life.

But if there is anyone that has to be blamed for the situation I am in right now, it is society and the old cultures themselves. My decision to avoid her and stop replying to her messages might have taken to make her adjust to a life in which I may not be present. But she must adjust to life without me when she loves me more because society won't accept our love. Society is so happy with the caste system and is unwilling to accept our love. We will soon be becoming the affected ones because of these, and when the times come, it will be difficult for her to understand. She is just sitting on a complex puzzle that, if it comes near, will only break her tiny little heart.

Now, if society had been so nice to us, if there is acceptance of love, then there would be no need for me to think about losing her happiness, as I could focus on getting better growth. When the time comes, I can go and speak to their parents because there will be no reason for they can highlight to reject me.

Her life is perfect before me, and I hope it is perfect now after I leave. I just wanted that the smile on her face remains with her, and whatever happens, she gets true love, at least from the new partner she had. I am moving on with my life, but I will be there for her whenever needed.

I failed to stand up for her one time. I know there will be no second one. But if the time comes when she needs someone, I promise that I'll stand for her this time, whatever in the world it may take.

The words I promised her, the promises I made to her, the wishes I have made in the temple to gods, and the dreams I have been dreaming all seemed to collapse at once. But in reality, I have been damaging all of these myself from the moment I stopped to ignore her, and I didn't even realize that those are being destroyed. So pity me. Now all the words that I have made failed to stand.

XIII

The unsent Letter

Dear Love,

You are such a marvellous feeling, and you make people go crazy. Crazy to go to any extent to get the things demanded of you. You can make people so powerful that they can do things that may look impossible to them before meeting you. You capture people's hearts, whomever it might be, and never fail to kick off everyone and everything from your heart to occupy your place there. Some call it permanent, and few call it temporary.

> *"You are a desire, you are a dream, you are a future, and you are destiny. People never think about anything when they have you. Maybe you are the world, and they forget everything they had thought of before."*

I even felt your powers. I was so deep into you that I forgot my dreams and career goal and became a slave to your magic. The life that you make people believe in makes you all leave everything. And I did. To get a beautiful life with her, I am ready to give up everything and anything.

I fell for your magic. I successfully got the Love of my girl and her acceptance, and we both together felt your magic. We stayed in your magic for a long time, and our bond grew stronger and stronger. We never wanted anything between us but to stay together forever as long as time and we exist.

But why do you have to be so discriminating among people? For some, you are heaven. For some, you are such a disaster that your effect has to be felt for life. It takes one's heart and soul to get you and the same to leave you.

Dear Love,

> "*Thank you for coming into my Love. Thank you for being with me. You made me understand life, people, myself, and society deeply.*"

We both fell for you and dreamed about our future of us together. You made our plans for the future look bright and beautiful.

And also made us realize many things. A big thanks for all those realizations. You make us realize that nothing is more important than someone who understands you; nothing stands when a person you love more enters your life. And nothing is more important than the smile of your loved one.

Everyone in society leaves on words. But when it comes to finding the reality on the ground, those words do fails to stand. I learned this late. And before I realize it, I am on my legs, struggling to stand straight.

You know what? Only the victim feels the real blow; here in my story am the victim, I am the villain, and I am the reason for both the start of Love and the ending of Love.

In my story, I created you and sowed the seeds for your appearance between us. It all started in my school days when the start was present. And from there, it grew, and one fine day it fell.

Dear Love,

Your story is a perfect hero and Villain type cinematic story every time. But not the real cinematic one, though, where the hero always wins. In your story, even the villain wins, and sometimes hero and villain are none but the same. And in some, you are the problem-causing catalyst.

In my story, I am a disappointing player. I am the culprit, and I am the fool. I never was a hero. But she is a real star and a girl of her word. OH love, if you really exist, be there for her. Make her new life and her new Love a success story. Let her win this time, bringing back all the hope she lost because of me. This time she cannot sustain another blow in her life. She might have already had the worst phase of Love.

If I ever meet her personally, I want to tell her Sorry. But that single sorry changes the entire story forever. It brings me back to her life. It becomes so complicated. A puzzle that is difficult to solve for two hearts deep in Love.

But I am writing you the letter I am supposed to send to her. Keep it with you, as I cannot keep these words inside my heart. Now it's time for me to let go. To go to distant places far from my reach. To explore the real truth of society, I need to go somewhere far to forget myself in the places.

Letter to Her

My dear,

I hope you have a happy new life. "I feel happy for you" is what I mentioned in my last message. But believe me, dear, I am suffering the pain I had never experienced. And the reason, as you know, is me. I am the reason for all the hell life you had for the past two years and the sadness in my life right now.

The situation is the end of our planned and dreamed future together. At least for me, the end is now. Maybe you accepted the end long back when you sent me the last message with a lot of pain in your heart and your words. I can sense the pain in your last words. But I failed to respond to those.

But believe me, I cried the hell out of me on seeing those messages, and I have no answer for why I didn't respond to you. I want to speak to you, but how can I when you block me? You changed all your numbers and email and blocked me on social media. There you are, cutting me from you in all the ways possible. I don't feel wrong from your end, dear. The mistake was and always is mine.

But I want to tell you sorry. When I last messaged you, I wanted to tell you many things, but backspace never allowed letters to be sent to you. I want to tell you sorry for everything that I have done. My heart and hands are not in coordination. A simple sorry might make me feel good, but I might damage your new life. I might create a new puzzle in your life. I might slowly drag myself into the hell that I am presently in. I don't want that to happen because all I ever tried was to make the smile on your face stay forever.

Dear, I wanted to speak to you as if my life is going to end now. If something happens and my life is at its last stage, the last wish I will have is to meet you and tell you on your face the real story and say SORRY. Look at your face and say goodbye to you and my life.

But even the words are becoming so complex for me. Everything becomes complex, even our own story. Why have I left you? I have no answer, dear. Maybe I am scared of my career. I have a dilemma about what to do when there is a clash between career and Love. I have to choose one. But then, I had no guts to face both of them and escape the confusion, and I followed the wrong path.

Dear, I have left you mainly because I am scared of this society. I cruel face of this society which I don't want you to face. When the time comes, everything will be black for our Love. Though we are happy at that time in our Love, we are supposed to face society, which will not end well for us. And I am scared of that thing.

I might have been a coward to hide from fighting, but I am not afraid to fight all those, but I am afraid of the result of those. I am scared of the defeat of our Love, and the biggest defeat I am scared of is seeing you lose your happiness and the smile on your face. I am truly scared of that.

Dear, I have failed in both.. both in my career and in my Love. So a career was never the reason for leaving you. Maybe not, I thought. And society had its role to play in my decision, but in the end, I made the decision.

Why did I leave you? I am scared of society. All the lecture that my mother has given me on that day has roots in my decision. And that had a huge impact on my life. I was so scared of the consequences in the future.

Not about the future that I am scared to fight, but about the future where you have to suffer. When you find it hard to move on with someone else forced by your parents, I didn't want that to happen and only wanted to make things easy for you.

But dear, I failed to understand or estimate the pain I would create in your life when I suddenly stopped messaging you. I failed, dear. I failed.

Sometimes hiding the real secret inside your heart and just a one-word message revealing how hard you are is what I keep telling myself. But this time, my heart stopped believing what my brain was trying to explain. It is just missing the feel and the touch of your hand.

Have a happy life, dear. If you feel lost at the end of the road, when in the case at any time, I will always be there for you, holding my hands wide open, my heart welcoming your arrival.

Until then, goodbye, and have a happy life. I hope the smile on your face remains as long as time and space exist, Dear. And forever and ever, I LOVE YOU.

XIV

Words do fail in Reality

Today I stand alone in my world, where my heart is crying hard, unable to forget her. Her smile, touch, and caring for me make me look back at the past and think of what I have done and hated myself.

How life has turned upside down for me. Right from her cute looks of her during my school days to the present smile on her face while someone else is tying the knot in her marriage. At both times, I stood there looking at her smile and my heart, just rejoicing at her smile.

All the words that I have told myself for the past years, right from my childhood, all the words that I have told her after I met her and all the words we together told each other, every word seemed like failed to stand now.

What I did for myself. What mistake have I committed in this life that I have to suffer? Maybe the one question I have to ask is why she must suffer. Did she commit a mistake by loving me so truly? Did she make a mistake in believing me blindly and hoping that I'll stay with her till the end? Why does she have to suffer for all the mistakes that I have made and all the mistakes society has made?

Maybe I'll never know the answer!

> *"Did people know that millions of hearts are just living a hell life, unable to forget their past love and move on with their present life? They are suffering because of the old historic rules which made the caste a centrepiece in all family decisions."*

Right from my childhood, morals have been considered an important thing to be taught to all children. I have seen elders speak about what is good and bad whenever we perform something. During all those speeches, why did they fail to teach us the morals behind the historical caste system and unwillingness to accept a person from another caste?

When two hearts and two souls are so deep in love, where does the cast come into play? If caste is so important in one's life, why is all of a person's childhood made to believe all the moral things of equality and truth? Did the elders do morally by not teaching the children about the cruel reality of society in terms of caste?

Can we take it that all the words taught to children right from childhood fail to stand when they become adults and face the real true society? When those words fail to stand.

Suppose they have taught me or someone suffering right now because they got separated only because they are from different castes. And if all of us might have known the truth from childhood, then maybe we had asked the caste of my love before I started to fall for her.

This looks so rude. We are asking a caste of a person before loving. This is like selecting a person from our caste, not someone we love. Believe my heart knows no caste and no religion, and the world though I realized this very long back, failed to implement it in reality.

As I stress on the line, The words fail to stand in reality. The words were spoken by me to my love, " ill stay with you forever" Failed to stand in reality.

> "*The words that were promised by my elders when I was a child, " You will get a person you love", Failed to stand in reality.*"

And the word my teachers spoke, " Caste and religion differences vanished in the society long back", Failed to stand in reality.

All stories are not supposed to end happily. But fantasies we are told from childhood always end on a happy note. Ultimately, the king and the queen come together and lead a happy life. The final words look so satisfying, right?

But real stories have both happy endings and sad endings. What about my story? Is it a happy ending or a sad ending? What type of words can I use to describe my life story?

Can I call it a sad story as both hearts who wished to stay together, who promised each other that they would stay together, failed to keep the promise, and now they are travelling on two different paths?

Can I call it a happy story because she has found someone, my wish to keep the smile on her face is succeeded, and all the pain she should have endured fighting against her parents and society is avoided with my foolish decision? My dream of keeping a smile on my face forever is achieved as she finds someone to keep her happy.

What words do I use? Do I use the words from my perspective or her perspective? From my side, I lost someone whom I loved, and I had a sad ending. From her side, she avoided some fool who just left the relationship in the middle and cheated and now that she has found someone who can keep her happy.

So even my story had two different perspectives, and I cannot use any words to describe it this time. For the first time, I truly realize that words have failed to describe reality.

The only words that still stand are " *I Love You Forever*", But your love will not stay with you as now she is gone with someone else. And as time passes, you can also find someone loving you more, and you are supposed to MOVE ON.

Our hearts May be or may not change the decision to love the person even if we are taught that we have to love only a specific caste person. The knot between two hearts and the caste system is very complex and difficult to understand. And even the heart fails to understand.

The story has turned upside down for me. It all started right when I was in my school when I told myself she was the one. I like how my entire school life comes before me, with only her role being a major part of it.

All the words that I told myself when she left. *I'll keep waiting for her. I'll achieve a good position to get back to her. All those words keep coming back to me now.*

What about Everything I told her when I started chatting with her?How cautious I have been and how many things I have told myself.

What about all the promises I made in the holy place, the temple we visited that day? All the words I have asked the god on that particular. All the words I have told her, like a promise that we will stay together whatever happens.

The words were spoken by her smile when I kept Kumkum on her forehead. Those millions of different words that smile spoke on that day, what happened to all those right now?

And in reality, the words fail to stand. Words spoken by individuals, words spoken by elders, words spoken by a lover, Words spoken by society, words spoken by your friends or relatives; Everything fails to stand, and it is very late before you realize those.

In reality, it is not the word which will succeed to stand, but the love and the heart that stays forever. With love in my heart for her and my wish for her to lead a happy life with her new partner, I rest my words here, as there will not be any end for all the words to be spoken. There is no meaning in getting all the words out, as I would like to feel the pain and suffering for myself for all the mistakes that I have committed and all the wrong decisions I have committed.

Thank you right from my heart for your time. The story is very close to my heart, and I hope I made you feel the emotion of love and the emotion of pain.

I tried to be as realistic as possible to bring to light the true reality of situations faced by youngsters when they had to choose between the girl they imagined their future and their family, which supported and responsible for all the beautiful past they had and without whom nothing should have been possible.

The dilemma is real, the scary decisions are real, and the suffering is real.

Signing off

Nikhil

Please share your valuable thoughts and feedback at the below link.

https://forms.gle/5KeFKRdqKCKvCchG9